What is She Doing Here?

Tales of the Trails of Annadel

By
Marna J. Stansberry

Dedicated to:
My late husband, Richard,
and to
My Father, Edward Johnson,
who told me,
"If you want to find God,
go out into nature."

"To him who in the love of Nature
holds communion with her visible forms,
she speaks a various language.

William Cullen Bryant

"What's the point of life
If you can't laugh a little?"

Louie Sambush, Aged 101

Foreword

A forward is a beginning. This one is the forward to an end. For the past few years I have been walking, hiking, and wandering on some of the trails in Annadel, a California state park. What a time I have had, enjoying every step, or almost every single step, as there may have been a few that were not pure pleasure. My hours in this park, observing, feeling and enjoying nature have been some of my best.

What am I doing here? Some are surprised to see this old person by herself on steep and sometimes difficult trails. The answer is I am having a fine time, trying to see as much of this beautiful place as I can.

One day, while walking at Spring Lake, I asked a county ranger a question. He answered and added that he remembered seeing me during his time working in Annadel. He said he stopped on the top of Richardson Trail upon seeing me, thinking, "What is she doing here? How did she get here?" When I told him of an old campfire I had seen up on Cobblestone Trail, he realized I hiked by myself in these hills. I have been told of others saying and thinking the same question.

Now I am past ninety years old. My eyesight is diminishing and I am slowing, losing balance and the ability to walk steep trails long hours. This little book is much smaller than I had planned, but the message would be the same if it were longer. I want to ask people, especially the older ones, to go outside into nature, onto the paths and trails, take time to know what is there, what you can learn while walking under tall trees or standing in a meadow, feeling grass blowing against your legs, watching a deer watching you. Few things equal the beauty of the early, rose-colored, velvety leaves of black-oak trees or the pure joy of spring sunshine reflected by the first buttercups.

While reading these pieces, I want you to feel and see what I experienced on each walk. When I go to False Lake Marsh and see those lovely, little white fritillaries, I want you to see those flowers, to hear with me wind blowing in the trees as I climbed there. Learn you have the strength to make the hard climbs through rock-covered hill trails. Try. You may find you can do it all. See everything around you. There is so much to observe. Never stop trying to learn.

Reflections

Walking in Annadel Park on a foggy September morning, I am struck by the dim light that makes the tattered, bleached, and broken grass look even paler. As I climb through a fir-studded hillside, I notice the gloomy light under the trees. Nearby, tall live oaks are adorned with moss, and long pieces of hanging fishnet lichen look gray.

Gazing upward through the trees, I search the foggy sky for a spot of blue. Ah, there it is, off to the east. I am cheered knowing that blue will soon cover the sky and the sun will be shining. The forest and I will feel all is right with this day, and the autumn yellow leaves of the big leaf maples will be glowing with light.

The beauties of this quiet forest have become such a large part of my life. I have wandered through the trails and hills of this lovely place, seeing it through many seasons. Looking forward almost every day to a pleasant time, whether a long hike or a short walk, with the happiness of being outside, under the trees with wonderful things to experience. There will always be something to look forward to seeing and feeling. I walk in familiar places, but every time is different.

I recall one day in May on the trail surrounding Lake Ilsanjo. A large black oak had fallen, blocking the trail, but hikers had forged a new trail around it. Following their path, I suddenly encountered a magnificent marsh filled with blooming white camas lilies. The marsh had standing water, and the lilies were much smaller than usual. Flowers bloomed everywhere; white lilies, pink shooting stars, fluffy yellow cream cups and golden sun cups. Such a glorious glowing field; I stood transfixed and took it in. There were blooming sun cups on both sides of the trail. There was an aged, bent oak, deeply covered with green moss, leaning toward the lake. The noonday sun reflected from the lake was a glittering contrast to the greens of the tree.

Continuing on, I saw lots of blue blossomed hound's tongue plants. Farther along the trail, under trees, in a shaft of sunlight, stood one perfect blue flower with a companion yellow buttercup. Both were surrounded by low-growing golden sun cups. I paused, thinking I'll never forget this.

In September heat I long for cooling rain, perhaps just a bit of drizzle and a wintry ramble through mud puddles and damp. I look forward to the freshening of the seasonal creeks, as in a day after a fall downpour they go from dry and dusty to water-filled streams. I think of North Burma Creek, which only runs in winter, but what fun it makes of it! Hurrying, tumbling, running from side to side on its way downhill. Bouncing off boulders and downed trees, following its worn bed, but making new dashes and eddies where earlier none existed. Each year it wears new paths, always striving to be bigger, wider and higher. The water always wants more.

Today I climb up Richardson Trail, seeing the dust as bicyclists race down on their way to the bottom. So much water drains out of this hill in winter, the trail becomes very muddy. I recall crossing from velvety leaves of black-oak trees or the pure joy of spring sunshine reflected by the first buttercups.

I look side to side, searching for drier places to walk. Now I cross back and forth, looking for shade in which to climb.

As I struggle uphill, slowly and carefully as always, I am passed by a young runner in a hurry. Soon he returns downhill. Time after time he dashes past me and then down again. I think he must be timing his runs. I admire his youth and agility as I regret my lack of both. I almost laugh aloud as I think of the contrast we make: me, struggling along in age with almost nowhere left to go and he, dashing along in youth, with so many places to go, so much to see and so much to do. I am smiling as I think of it and the young fellow, returning again, smiles back at me.

It is there: peace, beauty, comfort and, as yet, undiscovered treasures. To make yourself better, happier, go out there, walk, see and feel the beauty and wonder of the natural world while you are still able. Never stop trying to learn.

My Valentines

On February 14, I drive toward Annadel Park. It is cool and damp; my windshield is covered with misty drops of water. I plan to walk up Richardson Trail anyway; I am warmly dressed and there are lots of trees for hiding from rain. I hope my hat does not get too wet and droopy. I check water, lunch, camera, hiking sticks and me too. All of us are ready to go.

Starting the trail, I look carefully at the bank on my right to see what new things may be growing there. Here is a splendid growth of unusual lichen. I bring out the camera to discover the battery should have been charged. I forgot to check that. Lamenting the loss to posterity of a mossy masterpiece, I continue. There are slowly reviving goldback ferns not as green and vigorous as usual. Some fronds remain dry, withered, touched with brown and black. An occasional large drop of water hits my head. I wish these bits of tree-accumulated mist could all be redirected to the ferns.

At the entrance to Steve's S Trail I see how much water came through here during last weekend's storm. The accumulation of forest leaves, needles, twigs, sticks and small rocks on the trail have been washed downhill, making channels through the fire trail and across to the opposite bank. The underlying compacted soil and larger rocks are exposed with many big pieces of obsidian, a reminder this was a favorite place for Indian tribes to collect obsidian for spears, knives and arrowheads.

There is much fungus growing on pieces of trees and logs on this hill. Nearby, I see various striped and ruffled wood fungus. Something on a live tree catches my interest. An accumulation of fungus looking as if they might be oyster mushrooms. It is interesting, but not appetite-tempting for me. I am far too ignorant in the field of fungus. I see a few delicate gray mushrooms resembling little parasols. I think these are a kind of mycena and I admire their fragility. Higher on the hill I encounter another variety of this mushroom growing from a pile of horse manure. They are lovely in their pure white beauty, so fluted and thin they seem to glow.

The mist is gone and hints of blue light the sky. I walk down the hill, as there are other places I want to check. When I reach the parking lot, I turn right and begin Channel Trail. This is the third time I have searched this area to find a beehive I saw here last fall and summer. Easily seen from the path, it had been a perfect oval in shape, pale gray and handsome as it hung, attached to a tree, about twenty feet away. For the third time I see no sign of it, not even remnants, and leave a bit saddened. What happened? It was a pleasure to see, and I miss it.

Back on Channel Drive, I want to see a favorite fungus-viewing place. I discover two delicate lavender mycena mushrooms. The parasol top of one is starting to shred with age and the other, not yet opened, is pushing up through needles and leaves. I am delighted to see little white finger fungus proliferating all over this place. I was happy to make their acquaintance last year and am equally pleased again.

I go home thinking this has been an outstanding way to spend a Valentine's Day. No hearts and flowers but splendid fungus. How many people have that?

May Day

May Day! Ah, the festivities associated with this day. I might prefer picketing and protesting injustice, but think I must settle for a self-indulgent dance around the Maypole kind of day.

Every time I begin North Burma Trail, I think of the time I started this path and encountered a group of hikers carrying pails and shovels. I was told they were from the Land Paths organization and were there to do repair work. Glad to hear that, I stood aside and let them hurry on. A few parents were accompanied by children. One small boy with his father seemed a bit glum and, after walking about twenty yards up the trail, plaintively asked, "Are we there yet?" I smiled to myself as I thought "that father is in for a lot of fun today."

Above the trail is a small patch of scarlet Indian paint brush. A couple of years ago there were two plants. I count seven today and am delighted to see this increase, as I have liked and admired these flowers since I was a small child. My brother and I saw these as we walked and ran about in meadows and forests near the Eel River in Humboldt County during the early 1930s.

I cross the rough, rock strewn, now dry, creek crossing. Earlier this year, I tottered through water from rock to rock in my hikes up this hill. Today it is dry and dusty and the moss on the boulders is fading.

I stand aside to let a downhill runner I often see go past. She says, "I do this now so I can do what you do when I am your age." I say, "Continue what you are doing and you will do a lot more."

Farther up there are so many ferns and plants to see on the still-damp banks of this canyon that I find it difficult to remember to watch my feet. The trail is covered with loose rocks and I must concentrate as I climb. I compromise by advancing about three feet while watching my feet and the path. Stop, look up, look down, look all around so I do not miss anything, then go on. Sounds like advice for a small child, but it is helpful. I must remember my physical limitations, then plan and react accordingly. Frustrating? Annoying? Yes, but so is old age.

It is predicted to be hot today and very windy. The wind is blowing and moving the branches in the trees. The ground holds many fallen twigs, leaves, cones, and pieces of moss and lichen. I look forward to reaching the intersection with Live Oak Trail, but I can feel the temperature rising as the tree cover diminishes. Flowers still remain, but they are faded in color. A few buttercups persist near yellow lupine. The lupine is not yet in full bloom, though some flowers are starting to fade. It appears spring has rushed in, but is being crowded out by the arrival of summer. I like nice long, slow springs so I can enjoy every little sprig and blossom. I think of admonishing June and July to stop crowding, slow down, your time will come.

The manzanita trees show signs of age with many dead branches, though the trees are still a gorgeous red mahogany color with peeling bark. The bases are twisted, trunks and branches contorted and bent with gray and broken branches. Patches of lichen spread throughout the trees. I take several photographs so I can look at them and remember.

A jackrabbit dashes across in front of me. I stop, look and listen, hoping to get a better view of my fleet-footed little friend. No luck. He disappears into the underbrush.

I start into False Lake Marsh, which is flooded with sunlight. It is a very narrow trail and care must be taken to not step off as the trail-sides are crowded with small flowers. The meadow is breathtaking, carpeted with many colors and shapes of small blossoms. Entering, I am surrounded by bright-blue lupine with touches of white coloring their tops. Along the path are tiny pink and white linanthus. Yellow daisy-like goldfields scatter themselves through the meadow. They are joined by yellow butter-and-egg flowers, also short zygadene lilies, miniatures of full-size plants.

Now enter the stars of this wide meadow, white, first a few, then many. They are very small, only two or three inches tall and tinted with a pale blue. So delicate, so lovely, what a joy to see. I am happy and delighted I came. Reluctantly, I leave, careful not to step on the smallest part of all the beauty here.

The wind has become stronger and, as I descend trail, is more heavily littered with forest debris. One short, dead branch lands to the side. It is about two inches thick and two feet long. I think if it bounced off someone, it might be quite a shock. I meet a man coming up, and we exchange a few words about the wind and the heat of the day. We agree the wind makes it cooler down here, but it will be much hotter on top. Having just been there, I am now an expert on the heat of the hill.

As I continue, I am in and out of shade and look forward to a quiet bench farther down. Reaching it, I rest and consider what I have seen. The fellow I talked with earlier passes while going down, remarking on the heat, the wind and so on. Probably concerned about this old person, by herself, sitting on a lonely bench, he asks, "Are you all right?" I reply, "I am fine, having a good time and am very happy here." That seems to cover everything. He nods, smiles and departs. I sit for a time in great contentment before resuming the climb down the hill.

More to Come

The day after a light rain in early February, I go to Annadel wanting to see if the park looks better. I check the moss on trees and rocks by North Burma Creek. I think it looks a bit greener, though far from robust. On a shaded bank, I see the season's first leaves of maidenhair fern. Though late, they are very welcome. So far, just tiny, fresh green dots on black wire stems, looking delicate and charming.

The other ferns, refreshed and invigorated after earlier rains, seem less healthy now. The polyploidies are fewer than last month, this year's collapsed fronds almost indistinguishable from last year's. Even hardy sword ferns are drier, with limp and browning fronds, and the wood ferns are much diminished in vitality. The most affected are the goldback ferns. Starting after September's rain they unfurled, healthy and ready for life. After a long wait for more water, they folded to conserve energy for the next rain. A bit more damp came and they repeated. By the third time they were dejected, disillusioned, and prepared to give up. After refolding, they started to brown with many fronds and stems dying. Now they seem reluctant and slow to revive.

Walking on Channel Drive, I note that the tiny green plants by the road are refreshed. There are lots of foam flower starts and the soft leaves of chickweed are everywhere. Here and there are beginnings of miner's lettuce. The early leaves are narrow, but will widen soon, followed by those succulent circles of green. A good thing, as it would be sad to say sorry to a miner's need for salad.

Along the paving are washed patterns in fir needles showing how the water flowed off to the sides during the rain.

14

The surprising thing about the needles is that most of them are green. I don't remember this from last year and wonder if drought may have caused it.

Later, after a weekend's unusually heavy rain, I go in again along Channel Drive needing to see the changes in moss, ferns, creeks and trees. I want to check on my Annadel garden. Going in, I slow to see water dripping down a rock wall across from creek-side redwoods. When by the large wooden Annadel Park sign, I remember the low-growing bright-yellow sun cups that bloom around it in spring. With more rain, I have hope we will see them soon.

Anxious to see North Burma Creek, I hear it before seeing it. The sound is lovely, lively, and fine; and that is how it looks. It is now a good winter creek, running, rushing, hurrying into a wide culvert under the road and down to the larger creek below.

There are signs of an earlier overflow covering the road and causing damage to a lower, gated road, and traces of flowing water on creek banks and road edges. We had three days of unusually heavy rain, and some results are apparent here.

As I walk, I see a roadside covering of downed broken branches of varied size. Under the oaks, the ground is spread with lichen fallen from the trees during the storm. It seems littered with shattered pieces of gray. I notice cleanup has been done and is ongoing. The largest branches have been taken away from the edges and out of the creek. Work is continuing to clear the drainage ditches.

Checking shady places for ferns, I see many small new ones. The maidenhair is growing larger and the goldback ferns seem more robust. I encounter a large flock of wild turkeys and a cyclist photographing them. Soon they wander away into the bushes.

Creekside, below the road, a fir and a bay tree have fallen. It looks as if the fir took down the bay. They are fresh with the needled branches and long bay leaves mingling as they may have done when standing before the storm.

The moss on trees is richly green with the under moss sometimes topped by a longer, heavier variety, which curls and hangs in generous tufts. Ferns grow in this moss covering. High on one tree, several small branches are so deeply covered with long shaggy moss that a polyploidy fern is able to grow, seeming as if it is floating there.

Tiny roadside plants are thriving, though they will need more rain. The sun is now hidden by clouds and it is much cooler. I return to my car, start to go, stop when I see two deer about to cross the road. We regard one another, but they think I may be a menace and turn back into the trees.

I think of what I have seen on this wet, cool day. It is a lovely time of mud, damp and dark. Altogether fine, exactly right for a day in February.

Flower Fiesta

On May 5, I plan to hike up North Burma Trail to Live Oak, to Rough Go, then Lake Trail and return on Richardson Trail to Channel Drive.

I commence in my usual slow look-at-everything style, having to use care as there are boulders, large rocks and small loose rocks on this trail. The water and mud here is much diminished as is the water in the nearby creek. The stream at the bottom of the hill is quiet, but as I go up the sound of the water's steeper descent gives a refreshing background noise.

The climb is made easier by accompanying yellow lupine plants. I had worried about fording the creek and am relieved to find I make only small splashes when crossing. There is a large male deer, antlers still in velvet, standing quietly watching me. I emulate him and we each stand and stare. After a bit, we tire and go our separate ways. Finally, I am passed by two cyclists and am happy to see I am not alone in this dark, quiet canyon.

A bit farther up there are high damp banks covered and enhanced by moss and ferns. White meadowfoam plants and numerous woodland star flowers are blooming. I have never before seen so many of these delicate white stars in one place. Nearby are bright blue royal larkspur blossoms.

I start Live Oak Trail and have a brisk climb on the rutted, worn path. There are lots of cut rocks and chips from their cutting. Most of the rocks are in tumbled piles, but in one place they have been built into walls leading to what appears to have been a quarry. A more recent builder has left his mark, two neatly stacked spires of flat, cut rock topped with carefully placed stones of various shapes and sizes in a

17

presentation of balance.

Growing among, around and between the rocks are large daisy-like yellow mules ears, blue Douglas iris and blue-eyed grass. The flowers present a handsome contrast to the cut and broken dark rocks. Nearby is one fragile yellow fairy lantern in bloom. The stem is delicate, seeming almost too fine to support the little blossom. Along the path are flowers of many kinds and colors. I encounter more and more yellow lupin, finally entire thickets of it in full bloom with enhancements of blue-eyed grass. The edge of the path has bright pink and strangely named tom cat clover, tiny white and pink linanthus flowers and the yellow blooms of lotus.

At first the mixed oak forest continues, but then I enter large, grassy meadows where the principle trees are coast live oaks. One is the largest I have ever seen. The lower branches are so long and heavy they lie on the ground, then grow up again, as if taking root. I am amazed at the size and magnificence of the live oaks here.

Where Live Oak meets Rough Go Trail, a picnic table and benches stand under a tree. It's a welcome place to pause and view the meadows, trees, hills and valleys of Annadel

Park. Acres of blooming grass with many kinds of flowers cover the meadows. I enjoy seeing the blooms on flowers and grass and sneeze in appreciation as I go through the fields to the lake.

I stop to admire a small marsh filled with enchanting flowers of many kinds and colors. Small white camass lilies, bright-blue and white lupin, small yellow daisies and large, bright yellow helianthelia blossoms. There are so many shapes and colors, I find it hard to walk away from them. I leave and see the path edges are enhanced by the cheery yellow glow of flowers called sun cups.

Off this trail there is a gazebo built of stone and wood, an agreeable place to rest and think. It was given by the estate of Elmer Burke in 1984 and is dedicated to his memory. Staying for a while, I say thank you to that nature-loving gentleman and his family.

I meet two young men coming from Lake Ilsanjo, carrying fishing poles. I smile, say hello. They respond and one says, "Happy Cinco de Mayo." Laughing, I answer, "I had forgotten, Happy Cinco de Mayo to both of you." It is a friendly moment, and I feel energized starting up the first part of Richardson Trail.

Scarcely begun, I must stop and admire the hillside above. There are scarlet delphinium plants at the base with other flowers of white, yellow and blue. Deep-green bunch grass, dark basalt rocks, some with moss and lichen, seem to have been placed for display, and climbing around the rocks and over the hill are monkey flower bushes with yellow blossoms. I am having the joy of a Flower Fiesta in my own celebration of Cinco de Mayo.

Over the Top

I wanted to do something special to celebrate my eighty-eighth birthday, July 16, 2011, a small thing, but an accomplishment for me. What I most enjoy is hiking, so perhaps a nice, long, challenging walk. I had been thinking of going over the top of Annadel Park, from the eastside to west. Hike over the top? Over the top sounds good, better than it really is. The trails are steep, but it is only about four and one-half miles to where I want to go.

I planned the hike for the weekend before my birthday, as I like to hike when people are on trails that are difficult for me. As I age, the more I appreciate having others present during my little adventures, in case I may need help. I consulted a park trails map to decide on the most direct route, had familiarity with all the trails I would use and asked my daughter, Dorian, and her husband, Patrick, if they could take me back to where I would have to leave my car. Alarmed, she tried to talk me out of the idea. I assured her I had hiked all these trails before, just not across. She insisted her husband would meet me at Lake Ilsanjo and go down with me.

On a Saturday morning, I wake feeling lively and ready for an adventure. The heat is predicted to stay below eighty degrees, so I think this must be the right time. Driving to the park, I start up North Burma Trail. It is dusty and worn; the grass is dry and increasingly broken and disintegrating. Looking down to the bottom of the canyon, I see the green moss on the boulders is fading in the now dry creek. I climb, pausing to look for signs of the spring's flowers that grew here earlier. Occasionally, I find a cluster of dry leaves, but flowers have vanished until next spring. Near the dry stream crossing I discover the remains of a campfire, a very bad idea.

I climb to the place where last spring there was water drainage from the hill above and a beautiful display of plants and bushes in bloom. It is one of the loveliest places in the park. The flowers are gone, but a few ferns remain and cream bushes still hold white blossoms.

This is a rocky trail, and it is quickly becoming steeper as I climb its switchbacks. I travel slower and more carefully. Two young women come from below and say hello as they pass and hurry ahead. I admire their speed, glad to have others on this trail. Continuing the climb, at last I reach the start of Live Oak Trail where there will be open fields and big, beautiful coast live oak trees.

In spring, thickets of yellow flowered lupine grew here. So much is changed. Green leaves now have yellowing edges and flowers have become brown pods with falling seeds. After a short climb, I pass the remains of old quarries where San Francisco's cobblestones were dug and cut. The trail is uneven and full of small rocks and gravel-like pieces. I call these little rocks sliders and am careful when I have to walk and climb on them. The trails are worn, broken and covered with loose pieces, and I hike slowly, watching where I step. The sliders are one of many reasons I give myself an edge by using hiking poles.

Ah! Here is the meadow with great live oaks, beautiful, wide, dark shapes against the yellow grasses and blue sky. Nearing Rough Go Trail, I see the remains of a grass fire about a half-acre in size. It completely surrounds one of the largest trees and has singed the lower branches.

After the first turn on Lake Trail, I am surrounded by a lovely small meadow of lavender pennyroyal. Behind the pennyroyal flowers, the edge of the lake sports a rim of stiffly growing green reeds and in front, a ground-hugging trim of pink flowered lippia. Altogether a charming arrangement. I pick a leaf, inhaling the wonderful, healing, minty fragrance of that famous old herb, pennyroyal. Good for coughs, colds whatever ails you. Plant it in your garden and you will feel better, whether you are drinking its tea, smelling its goodness, or just having it near. A native Kentuckian once told me there is a county in that state named Pennyroyal, but the old-timers, in the early English way, still call both county and plant penryal.

I see Canadian Geese swimming in Lake Ilsanjo and then the entrance to Spring Creek Trail. I am not quite ready to face this downhill climb. Every time I go this way I think "never again." So, here I am again, muttering to myself, "Not again." As I commence, my spirits are lifted by the sight of two pearly everlasting plants I saw last time, now joined by more. Some of them, unusually tall, blend their white blooms with those of a dark-green toyon bush, covered with its own bouquets of fluffy white flowers.

This part of the trail hugs a steep, rocky wall with a precipitous canyon and a creek at the bottom. The trail is narrow, rocky, and rutted, covered with broken rock; all in all, a real treasure of a trail. I meet a young man, climbing up. He is pushing his bike, shirtless, and he is perspiring. He says he is new here, gave up trying to ride and is just walking and pushing his bike and how far to the top and aren't there better ways and, and....

I agree it is too hot, too steep, too difficult and tell him about Richardson Fire Trail, which I think is much easier for bicycles.

I realize one of the reasons I like hiking these trails is because it is a social outing. Almost everyone I see says hello, and many of the people are the same every time I go.

The cyclists are friendly and, though they all look alike to me in their helmets and racing outfits, some seem to remember me or, maybe, it's my fine old hiking hat they recognize. Most of them are polite and helpful, sometimes, not so much. There are rules for order on the trails: horses are first, hikers second, and bicycles rate last.

A few yellow flowers remain on the monkey flower bushes. Here and there are some large leaves of mule ear plants turning yellow and brown, but no more flowers bloom where  there were so many in spring. The trail is deeply rutted with few flat places and sometimes the only flat on this narrow trail is the canyon edge, so it becomes a pleasant exercise in balance. I decide the many clumps of poison oak would break a fall.

It is hot in the afternoon sun and becoming hotter, so I take frequent water breaks, always looking for a bit of shade. I see a shady trail ahead and am soon under trees. Two women walkers stop and ask if I am afraid, alone, if I always do this and so on and on. They are pleasant, friendly people, but surprised and, I think, concerned about my safety and sanity.

The Vietnam Veteran's Trail is the exit for this over-the-top hike, and I am out to my daughter's home nearby. There I am greeted by a glass of ice water and questions about why I didn't call. As always, she forgives my forgetfulness and we spend a refreshing time in their lovely garden. A light, cooling breeze is blowing as we sit and watch the birds and squirrels at the baths and feeders. The best part of the day is my feeling of thanks, peace, and enjoyment.

Trial by Rock

In late August, I walk toward the Vietnam Veteran's Park. After entering, I go to the left and descend down a rocky trail to a crossing of Spring Creek and into Annadel Park. This entry is short, but steep and worn.

When I first saw it a few years ago, I thought there is no way I am going there. Since then, I bought hiking poles and practiced and have gained confidence. Still, every time I attempt this slip-slide slope I think, at age 88, I may have taken leave of good sense. I admire young people trotting up and down this bank. Ah, the carefree confidence of youth.

In the sandy soil of a former creek there are many yellow-flowering buffalo burr plants. The burrs on these plants are formidable. Nearby is a stand of lavender blooming pennyroyal. Climbing up the other side is not as steep, but has many opportunities for sliding. I am relieved when I reach the flat, wide fire trail above. Blooming along the trail are Fitch's spikeweed plants. The yellow blossoms are pretty, but the rest of the plant is well named.

I cross the bridge that leads to Canyon Trail. As you go up, the hill is on your right. On the left is a steep canyon with a boulder-filled creek bed at the bottom. In the winter there is a fine, noisy creek down there. Now it is so dry, I cannot see even one puddle.

The hillside, both above and below, has lots of beginner poison oak as well as many tall stands of it, now almost bare, but here and there a few red leaves hang on, brightening the parched grass. Some of the vines have climbed into trees where their color glows brighter against the green leaves.

The rocky trail is tired, dusty and worn. What appear to be bristles only three or four inches long occasionally protrude from the path. They are remnants of roots, still attached, but so worn, the only portions remaining are these tough fibers.

Most of the trail here is roughly covered with rocks, large and small, including pieces of round and oblong pillow-like lava. There are small areas of dirt, sand and sandstone, and a white powdery substance so fine it looks like ash. I find it endlessly fascinating to see so much lava and places showing the results of volcanic explosions millions of years ago. The rocks and soil are interesting, but it is difficult walking, and I search for flat places. Crossing from side to side, I look both ways for cyclists, runners and hikers.

A bench with words carved into the back, *Tom's Trek Stop*, presents a touch of humor on the trail. I like to rest here, just above the trail, to enjoy the views across a small valley to the Bennett Valley hills and, even farther, to the coastal hills. Today, there is a layer of dense gray fog running along the coast with a contrasting fluff of small white cumulus clouds above.

Between this bench and nearby hills are white patches where no vegetation grows, resembling the white rock and powder on the trail. Above is an old oak tree with many dead, leafless branches, a furrowed gray trunk and at its base, the remains of a blasted and broken long-dead oak. Higher on the hillside are buckeye trees, leafless, the crooked, silver-gray barked branches drooping down, like long white hair straggling toward the valley below.

When higher on the trail, I stop to see the wide view of Santa Rosa and the expanse beyond. I stand here to look at the mountains that march northward, colored blue by distance. Closer, Spring Lake is seen through the trees in a valley below.

I go down again and return to a damaged section in the fire trail. Water, rushing through here in the winter, created a channel, exposing large rocks and making a difficult gulch to cross. I do it with care and continue downhill.

I hear a bike behind me and a boy of about twelve speeds past, skids to a halt, almost falls, but jumps clear as his bike goes down. On the lower side of the trail is a foot or two of cleared space in the brush and an eroded rut for winter water. The boy mounts his bike and heads down there. Again, almost falling, he gets off and, pushing the bike, proceeds down the rough hillside. He is soon hidden by brush and I am left wondering, where he is going, why this dangerous way down a steep hill? When reaching the level below, I find the young boy had taken an illegal shortcut, posted with warning signs. Thinking the little fellow not a charming lad but an obnoxious twit, I proceed on my way.

Farther down, I am at the side of the canyon when I hear bikes coming fast behind me. I move as near the edge as possible. A biker whizzes past, so close I feel the rush of air as he speeds by. He is so intent on being first, he did not even seem to see me. Two others, behind him, wisely stay near the middle. This is the closest any bike has ever come, and I feel fortunate to not be in the canyon below.

When returning to Canyon Bridge, I see an almost hidden, low-growing group of plants, so dust covered the exact shape and color of the leaves cannot be seen. Though the flowers are dusty, I can still see the brightness of the red flowers and decide they are California fuschias.

I return by way of the back trail to the Vietnam Veteran's park. It is a narrow, rocky way cut into a steep hill posted for no bikes or horses. I have sometimes met a cyclist, though never a horse. I like it because, in spring, the hill is covered with blooming bushes and flowers. You do have to ignore the rivulets of water running down the trail and concentrate instead on the colors and shapes of the flowers. Now, flowers are gone, grass is dry and trees and bushes are browning, starting to lose their leaves. Near the bottom, plants are still getting some water from hill drainage so have remained green. As I go up, I see autumn is coming first to the top of the hill. The buckeye trees have lost their leaves and only retain some of their large seed pods. The pods on the ground are opening to release more seeds. These outsized nuts are somewhat poisonous. Indians chopped them into pieces and put them in stream pools to stun the fish for easy harvesting. Some oaks have browned. Their leaves are coming down. The trailing fishnet lichen is again on display on this windy hill.

I think of Canyon Trail and this as trial by rock. Why do I come here if I complain? The answer may be I want to see it all.

Songs of Spring

There is lots of sunshine on this March day, clear and bright with a cold, sharp wind. I zip my coat and pull my friend, the Hiking Hat, down on my head to secure it. On windy days I have a fear of chasing this fine-old straw hat down, around, and off the trail. I have both spring fever and hay fever today and, as I start up the Vietnam Veteran's Trail, thinking of all the tree pollen I will encounter is not helping. Going by a heavily laden, blooming live oak tree brings on a large sneeze. I start humming "Oh, What a Beautiful Morning," and start uphill.

This small memorial park has several benches on which to sit and enjoy the view of Santa Rosa and the canyon and hills behind. Lots of trees and green grass make it a pleasant place for contemplation. Here the grass is enriched with bright bursts of color; white popcorn flowers, buttercups and orange fiddlenecks, blue dick blossoms, tiny lupines, purple vetch, and pink shooting stars. So much, so lovely, it is a feast of colors and shapes.

I walk downhill, closer to the entrance and take a trail that leads to the canyon behind, then across to the entrance to Annadel Park. As I go down the hill, I see a purple sanicle and scarcely believe it. There are none yet in bloom on the east side of Annadel Park. Nearby is a wild cucumber in full flower, growing and starting to cover its side of the hill and everything within reach. There are little pink spots in the grass and as I move closer, I see many plectritis blooms. The lovage plants are blooming too. None of this is happening, as yet, on the other side of the park. Is it the western sun, or is this the test kitchen for Annadel flowers?

By the side of the trail leading to Canyon and Spring

Creek Trails, there is an old rock wall that seems to have been the foundation for a long-gone building. I sit there while making notes of the flowers I saw today. Not far away is a piece of another wall, moss and fern covered. Standing over it is a large cream bush, waiting for its turn to bloom.

The bottom of this canyon holds a stream that sometimes is no more than a trickle, at other times, dry. Today it is real; it is Spring Creek and proud of it. It comes rushing and roaring down from the hills, bouncing off rocks and trees. I hear it singing and shouting, "I am river, hear me roar." Impressed, I stop to watch and listen. Today this little creek has the sound of a strong mountain stream.

I decide to walk up Spring Creek Trail if it is not too muddy. It looks like some good gravel work has been done, and I am able to avoid mud and water most of the time. I sit down on a long downed tree in a sunny clearing and gaze at trees, creek, ferns, grass and what is this? Tiny, pink plectritis plants, only two or three inches tall, cover the ground near me. Usually they are taller, but these are minis and so close together they look like pretty ground cover.

Feeling tired and chilled, I return, cross the bridge and look at Canyon Trail. Today it seems to be a muddy, rock-filled jumble. I turn and go up the canyon side of the Vietnam Veteran's Trail and find myself encircled and entranced by buttercups. In front, in back and on both sides, trimmed with occasional blooms of blue eyed grass, they cover this part of the hill. Flowers accompany me as I climb. Here and there the narrow path looks like a small stream bed. There is nothing to be done, but trudge through the water and enjoy the lovely views on all sides. New leaves on the trees, fresh green grass, lovely flowers and a noisy creek below make it memorable.

Nearing the top, I see a new flower and realize I am looking at white phacelias. Unusual, pretty curled flowers. I think these lovely flowers with such an unusual name should have a song. I start with, "Oh, Phacelia, sweet Phacelia, I dream of you on winter nights, my Phacelia." Thinking my song lacks more than a bit of everything, I give it up and go to a bench to admire the view.

A turkey vulture flies low over the edge of the hill. Catching the uphill wind, it suddenly soars in ever-widening circles, higher and higher above me. Joined by two others, they use the wind, dipping, soaring, circling high and down, into the wind and away, enjoying the strong drafts. Entranced by the grace of their wings, making dark patterns against the blue sky I realize, as they are playing with the wind, I have been growing much colder while sitting in it.

Leaving I hear piercing bird cries from a nearby tree. There is a large tan and white bird sounding and looking fierce as it pursues something in that tree. It gives one last, loud, angry squawk and flies away. I watch as it flies and think I may have seen a Cooper's hawk in hunting mode.

"What a Day This Has Been, What a Rare Mood I'm In" is the song as I leave, wondering how soon I can come back.

Farther

Iwalk up Richardson trail on a sunny Sunday morning in March thinking I will go to the first bench to enjoy the pleasant view, but no more. It is rather late and warm for a long hike. Seeing a short Oregon grape bush with bright yellow blossoms, I remember it as always startling in its shining green and yellow. Farther up on the right is a large fir tree in the firm embrace of a giant poison oak vine. The vine is so thick and strong, the tree is indented by its clutch.

I reach the bench, admire the view, and think I'll go a little farther as I want to look at some redwoods, be in their shade and enjoy their fragrance. I am soon in deep shade and keep on climbing, admiring the trees, the moss and the ferns.

I stop at a favorite place where there is an elderly black oak, now shattered, heavy broken limbs on the ground. Part of the old tree trunk and a partially downed branch are still living and leaf out each year. I admire such determination in old age. Among the nearby leaves and grass there are two spots of blue Douglas iris. This spring everything seems a little early.

I decide to walk to the next rest spot as I might see more early blooms. Pausing at a picnic bench for a drink of water, I think about the budded camas lilies I saw last week. They are only a short way up the trail. I really want to see what they are doing and if they are well. So off I go and worth it, too, as those white lilies are blooming and a delight. Having gazed for a while, I think of the field up the trail that has many more and decide to go look.

I seem to have entered a failed logging operation. The park had to cut many dead fir trees and left them where they fell. It is natural, as these trees are old and rotten and will decompose. However, at this time it looks as if loggers, having finished their operations, departed without their trees.

Some of the grassy banks are sprinkled in pink. A closer look shows shooting star flowers, busy being pretty. There are occasional touches of white milk maids and, in partial shade, some blue blossomed hound's tongue flowers. Soon there are everyone's favorites, buttercups.

Turkeys strut across ahead of me. As always, they seem self-important and ludicrous. What is it about them? Is it their shape, their walk? They always make me smile. They act conceited and obnoxious but still amusing. Can it be they remind us of some people?

I notice bracken ferns are opening. I see a deer grazing on a hill above me. Ah, I think, just an average day in lovely Annadel. Lucky me, I came farther.

I stay for a few minutes at the bench at the top of this trail with its lovely view of Lake Ilsanjo. The view is better than last year and I wonder if, while cutting trees, bushes were trimmed a little to widen the sight of the lake. Tired, I resolve to turn back as soon as I have seen the camas lily field. I see the lilies are in bloom, though it seems perhaps fewer in number than in earlier years. Most are blooming far to the back, growing against a fringe of coyote bushes at the rear of the oak-filled meadow.

Finally, I say, "Enough!" to my wandering self and start back, stopping to admire a fine view of a flat area near the lake. Perhaps it is a marsh in rainier years. The field is gray and, at this distance, any underlying green grass cannot be seen. Occasional rounded boulders look like grazing cattle. I see a deeply cut sharp-edged gully with water sparkling in the bottom going from this hill across the fields to the lake. A busy seasonal creek runs by Richardson Trail traveling downhill. I try to remember if it goes to that gully. I would like to see, but no, it is too late, too far, and if I go down I will have to climb back up. The thought of that climb turns me in the other direction.

Walking downhill, enjoying the flowers in the grass along the trail, I stop to enjoy lilies, check the health of wild raspberry bushes, review any rocks and rills that come to sight, and wonder why it is so warm in March. I stop to rest by that old black oak and sit on a nearby bench. To my surprise there is a camas lily growing and blooming under the bench. I hope no one steps on it.

As I near the bottom there is a tiny white blossom against green leaves, a meadowfoam flower, quite alone, its five white petals and dark stamens peering from the lacy green leaves. A few feet farther down I see another, and then three more. Next week, many will be blooming and I will be back to enjoy their small perfection.

I meet a young woman and a very small boy. He is a beautiful, bright-looking child about two years old. He stops, says hi; I stop and say hello. He stands in front of me and, looking at me with big, dark eyes, begins a conversation. He does not yet have words, but he does. He looks at me, he gestures, uses inflections of voice and, with his own language, makes his meaning clear. We talk for a while. He comments on my walking sticks, I, on his curly dark hair. He asks where I've been, I tell him about the flowers and trees. It is time to go. He pantomimes kissing, so I kiss his lovely, soft curls, then he turns and starts downhill with me. The young woman takes his hand, we wave goodbye and I continue down as they go up. I think of all the wonderful, lovely things I have seen today. This beautiful child is the very best. I walk on out, tired, but grateful to have had this day.

Sunshine and Mud

A sunny Saturday presents itself. There are many people in Annadel Park enjoying the sunshine, exercising and admiring nature. I plan a short walk, the length of Channel Trail, to visit a little wildflower garden appearing each spring by two of the former quarry pits.

Near the entrance a stream of water is running downhill and overflowing the trail. The path in this section has been much improved by a paving of rock from the bounteous piles left by the quarrymen who cut the cobblestones here many years ago. In order to cross this path I must wade a bit, but it is solid and secure. The path uphill is wet and muddy, crossed with exposed tree roots and rocks. All those give many secure places to step when climbing. The path leads through poison oak, berry brambles and bushes to a clearing where there are two pits and piles of cut rock.

This is a remarkable springtime garden and, as always, I am delighted at the number and diversity of flowers. Coming uphill, I was surrounded by flowering lovage plants. They are increasing each year, spreading into the bushes and down the hill.

There are purple sanicles in bud, and orange fiddle-necks, blue ookows and white yarrow flowers, all blooming together in the abundant green grass. The latest and loveliest to bloom are blue royal larkskpurs. Again, I am happy to find so many bright pink shooting stars with their touches of black and white, flowering and flourishing on this soon to be summer-dry hill. Today it is so wet the water is sheeting downhill and running in rivulets, surrounding and soaking the path. It causes puddles and mud and mess and flowers to bloom, so I am happy to walk through the water.

Thinking I see tiny touches of lavender-pink in the grass, I must get down close enough to identify them. Blue-eyed Mary flowers! They are the smallest I have seen, perfect in every way except size. I see one extra small pink plectritis accompanied by an even smaller flash of pink, possibly a lotus. I pass into a more shaded area where there are many woodland pea vines and, finally, one in delightful pink and white bloom. I walk slowly looking for flowers and avoiding mud as best I can. It is such a lovely sunny day that avoiding the water amounts to just fun and games.

I reach North Burma Creek and see it, too, is having a fun-filled day. I go down to the road. No hikers attempt to cross the creek here today. All the bikers peddle on through, perhaps to prove strength, bravery, and a touch of that old derring-do. When I consider it, I think few of today's young people have heard of that last vintage virtue.

Going uphill to resume the climb on the other side, I am surprised by how wet and slippery it is. Again, exposed tree roots and rocks are the hiker's helpers. I clamber up with my poles, though I find myself slipping now and then. Mud in the path is abundant. The many bicycles passing through here cut and churn the dirt and forest duff into a thick, black, sticky mess. I try to stay on the edges. Sometimes none are left, so I pick a section looking less deep with sludge, and muck my way through. Not far from this mess is a lovely bed of blooming Indian warrior plants. Their ferny leaves and fluffy red flowers lighten the shade under the trees. I feel a bit more benevolent toward the mud and muddle on.

This is a familiar walk where I come often as it is easy, always pretty, and a fine place for a short, fast trip and a nature fix. As I balance on the slightly drier edges of puddles and mud, I look for the woodland star flowers that grow here.

It is too early, so far no sign of those thin-stemmed, fragile white beauties.

The maidenhair ferns are having good times. They seem to be happily healthy with no sign of the reluctance to grow they showed earlier this year. I welcome them with a soft pat and words of appreciation.

I enjoy the sun-brightened ferns and moss covering this hill. Everything looks green and glorious. Last month this place looked faded and dry, not at all its usual wet winter display. I feel happy to see all the beauty now, and wonder how it will look this summer, later this year. And how about next year?

Too Hot, Too Far, Too Tired

In early April I walk up Richardson Trail at ten in the morning. The trailside is full of small blooming flowers, principally miner's lettuce and foam flowers with buttercups and an occasional iris higher on the hill. It is a quiet walk as there are not many hikers or bikers out on this weekday morning. It is predicted to be a very warm day.

There is dampness at the lower edge of the bank where water drains from the recent rain. Along this edge the low-growing creeping buttercups are blooming, and I am happy to see these fresh-faced small flowers. They are joined by lots of cut-leaved geraniums with delicate pink flowers.

Advancing through a heavily wooded section, there is a seasonal streambed coming down the hill with mossy rocks and unusually large sword ferns. There are redwoods and, as always, I feel happy and peaceful among these trees. There are more and more tall yellow violets called Johnny Jump Ups and blue Douglas iris as I go up the hill. As the morning grows warmer, I appreciate the shade and think how nice it will be when returning this afternoon.

At the next resting place a cyclist is stretched full length on top of a table performing what seem to be back-stretching exercises. I can relate as my back feels it would be a good idea. Seeing me, he stands, then sits and shares the rest stop. We exchange a few words, and he inquires if I am going all the way to the lake, and wishes me a good hike. I wish him a good ride.

I walk along the final stretch to the top where blue lupine with buttercups and purple vetch grow in the grass near the trail. Along the edges are tiny plants with flashes of many colors. I marvel at the small size of some and the minutely perfect flowers. Everything is a joy in the sun-filled morning. The black oak meadow is gorgeous with creamy white lilies and blue iris in the bright spring grass. Such beauty is unforgettable.

Finding the sun warmer, I am glad to enter the shady walk leading down to the lake. As always, the fir trees and ferns on this hill and the flowering plants and cream bushes on the damp bank are pleasant.

Here is my first sighting of a little plant called Modesty, a low-growing creeper with pretty, opposite leaves and fluffy white flowers. With my flawed camera techniques intact, I take a couple of pictures and hope for the best.

After stopping to admire some scarlet delphinium blooms, I reach Lake Trail. My favorite lunch bench, with its view of the lake, is in the heat of the noonday sun, so I go into Lloyd's Trail. I am dazzled by the number of bright yellow sun cups scattered in the meadow. California poppies growing with them give more color.

There is a rocky climb ahead before connecting with North Burma Trail. It is growing warmer, and I look for a place to rest and eat lunch. I try the first likely rock and find it is too sunny. Climbing a bit, I find another, and it is too low. Feeling like Goldilocks, I give up and walk on. I am happy to see a gathering of blue-eyed Mary flowers. Who called this a seldom seen flower? In an open area, I see what can only be lomatium plants. I have been looking for these, and have misidentified them a couple of times. These are really the right ones. Of course, they are. Aren't they?

I enter a continuation of a small black oak forest that grows up and over this hill to the top of Richardson Trail, where the white lilies are blooming. The hillside is covered with a type of fescue called bunch grass. The clumps of dark green, coarse grass are now in flower, with tall wands of blooms waving over the hill.

I encounter a few puddles and teeter on the edges as I go by. Ceanothus bushes covered with bright blue flowers surround me as I turn on North Burma Trail. I find a just-right rock, sit, take out my lunch and get comfy. A young girl cyclist comes up the hill and seeing the bumps and rocks ahead says, "I hope I don't fall." I answer, "Call, and I will come to your rescue." Nothing more is heard, so I assume she gets through safely. A girl hiker walks by and stops to talk a bit about the hike and speeds of walking and some of the trails. We compare notes and she continues on. As I rest, I am looking at my surroundings, and see on the hill above me two yellow-blossomed monkey flower bushes.

Remembering a wide meadow ahead, it is so warm I dread the hot sun. I see two plants of daisy-like, yellow mule ears. Each plant has semi-collapsed in the hot sun and is leaning toward the ground. Not cheered by this, I venture into the meadow and plod on. To my relief, this stretch is not as wide as I remember, and soon I am under trees again and climbing toward an intersection with Richardson Trail where I turn left to go back to the beginning.

I go back and forth across the broad fire trail seeking shade and, as I go, I weigh whether the amount of shade is worth the effort of crossing. It grows warmer, and I am plodding until I reach a steady amount of shade and a bench to sit for a while. The trail will be in shade the rest of the way and it is all downhill.

I march on down and soon see a large male turkey in full-feathered array has taken possession of the road. He does not seem to want to leave and I, too tired for feathered nonsense, stalk ahead. He rattles his feathers a bit. I rattle and bang my metal hiking poles. I think, Bird, give me trouble and I will pound you down to a turkey sandwich. Pondering those poles, he saunters away to pay a call on one of his many admirers. He retreats and I proceed.

Summer Solitude

As I start an August walk up North Burma Trail, I see everything is dust covered. Surrounding grass is dry and broken. If I hit it with a stick, dust may float out. I see a nearby bent and withered clump of wild onion stalks with dark, open seed pods. All the seeds have fallen. Grass along the path is one color, buff. Edges of the path are littered with old leaves, twigs and sticks. Moss in the creek bed is shrinking and yellowed. Even the moss on the trees looks thin and dry. All are waiting for rain.

The beige and brown colors are occasionally disrupted by the red jewel tones of autumnal poison oak. Their foliage is gorgeous, whether in the dry grass or climbing trees. There is a cluster of small dead firs, broken branches support-

ing the scarlet-leaved vines that climb through the soft gray lichen-covered limbs. Nearby stands a young fir tree, fuzzy and green, a reminder of Christmas.

Deeper into the canyon, tired grass is replaced by more rocks, boulders, steep banks and bushes. Only in the deepest shade does moss retain some of its life and color.

In contrast with the dry ground, the trees keep their

bright leaves. Black oaks have a few colorful spots, here and there a spray of gold shining against the deep greens of the forest canopy. Evergreen bays add yellow and russet leaves to the ground.

Not far from the trail, a small live oak gives support to a honeysuckle vine that has happily climbed around and over the little tree. The vine carries its summer crop of translucent red berries. The curling vine and red berries are lovely against the dark tree leaves.

I reach the former creek crossing. Last winter it ran so fast and high, I was afraid to cross. Now it is a worn dirt path through boulders, rocks and pebbles. I am concerned by how dry this creek has become. I seat myself on one of my preferred park benches and look up to the place where last winter the creek came tumbling and rushing down the hill, bringing a litter of tree trunks, branches and sticks, testaments to the winter force of this seasonal stream. I have not seen it on any maps, but I always think of it as North Burma Creek.

This still place in quiet, deep shade is soothing and a comfort. I remember in winter the watery clamor of the stream. The walls of the canyon are close, and the dashing, bumping, rolling din echoes. I recall the water pounding off rocks and filling this place with sound. Now, in the quiet, what I hear is much diminished, peaceful and refreshing. There are occasional bird cries, twitters, a snatch of song, the shriek of a jay, and now the pounding of a woodpecker beating its beak against a tree. Ferns fill the hill behind me, rustling close and vying with poison oak for proximity to visitors. Wood ferns are doing well in this cool, shade covered, almost damp spot.

It is time to leave, but I choose to linger, appreciating the solitude and peace of this, my favored summer retreat in my favorite park. 🌲

Walking With Feeling

One wintry day in late January, I enter Channel Drive and see California bay laurel trees in bloom. A recent storm had broken a large branch of a bay tree which partly filled the road. Crossing, to look at the flowing creek below, I see it is much higher and muddier than last week.

I am happy to see and hear a recently freshened seasonal stream gurgling beside and under the road as it hurries down to the much larger creek. It approaches one of my favorite spots, a high sandstone wall by the road, the ferns growing there revived, happy for the water that oozes from the rock.

A monkey-flower plant seems pert and pleased as are the polypody ferns growing above. I stand still, feel the cold, and breathe in the dampness under the redwood trees by the creek. Noticing the inside edge of the road has been recently cleaned and trenched, I hurry to see if all the nightshade plants are gone. Only two or three remain. I hope they make it through the winter to grow their pretty white blossoms and black berries again.

I go to a roadside Garry oak to see if it is presenting any of its beautiful early leaves. Unlike some oaks on the western side of the park, it is abiding by the seasons and waiting its turn. The bare branches are striking against a nearby redwood with blue sky behind.

I hear the second little winter stream before I see it. This one has always been lively. It comes down, unseen, through a blackberry patch, to rush noisily over rocks and into a culvert to join the lower waterway. I wait quietly and listen for birds and the sound of disputatious crows comes loudly across the distance. Loud, impassioned arguments, full of sound and fury, meaning nothing, end when the birds take flight, climbing and whirling above the trees. A third small winter creek murmurs along, refreshed and enlarged. It, too, goes under the road, then slows, wandering across a field. Nearby, a small black oak, a child among trees, has its branches festooned with fishnet lichen.

Suddenly, the sun seems brighter and, pausing, I feel its warmth through my coat. Enjoying the sunshine, I notice I am walking beside a tangled mass of California wild roses. The canes look dead, with only a few presenting new leaves. I remember last spring's infestation of ugly red beetles and fear most of the roses may be dead.

Above the road, on the side of the hill, is one of my favored places for flower viewing later in the year. I remember the lovely wild white hyacinth growing in one of the pits made by earlier rock excavations. On the hillside there is water, slowly spreading over and dripping from a large, flat boulder. I hear sweet bird chirps, then the rush of passing cyclists, their tires swishing on the paving.

I enter a darker, damper place where tree branches meet overhead. The black paving holds a mixed salad of broken branches, moss, lichen, leaves, and forest detritus. I see the remains of a flattened newt, made almost transparent by the passing cars and heavy rain. I hear the voices of an approaching mother holding a sleeping baby, the father pushing the empty stroller.

Here is what I came hoping to see, my favorite small stream, unruly as always, rushing down beside North Burma Trail with large moss-covered rocks guiding its course. It, too, is channeled under the road and hurries out the other side, skirting a stand of oso berry bushes. I remember the early spring fragrance of their white blossoms. After entering a shadier place where the trees are denser, I note that last year's sick madrone tree is now dead. Grey-white leaves litter the ground. Nearby is another one, very small, and it, too, is dead, though the grayed, wrinkled leaves still cling to its branches. I think of sudden oak death disease and wonder how many trees may die in the park this year. Last season this bank held blooming Philadelphia fleabane plants, and I look forward to more blooms this year. I pass by three small fir trees, and one is dead, completely covered in lichen. The second, half-dead, is half encrusted. The next, even less covered, seems to be the healthiest. Under dense shade of much larger trees, they struggle to survive, and I don't think they can. It grows colder, so I turn and start out of the park.

Near the ranger station I hear bird chirps coming from a thicket of dormant poison oak. Just as I locate it, the bird flies away. It may be a female robin. I should learn more about birds, but my mind is too cluttered with plants to have room for birds, too. Down the road two turkeys are foraging. When they see me, they hold a conference and, deciding I present a threat, turn and scurry up a hill.

Behind me I hear the happy giggles and cries of a small child. I turn and see a mother and father with their little girl. Seeing me, she cries "Grandma!" We laugh and, flattered, I go on my way.

Winter's Rewards

Winter walks present special challenges, muddy trails holding streams of running water and puddles, lots and lots of puddles. With the difficulties come special pleasures. Ferns seen only in winter are one. In dry seasons, when passing shady, moss covered walls and banks, I remember the polyploidy ferns. When they start their rainy day life they stand upright, reaching for more damp. As they near complete size, they turn and start leaning down. As they grow to full length, they will appear to be coursing green waterfalls waving down rocks and walls of the forest. I look forward to their appearance every winter and regret their departure. When seeing the early signs of them this year, I began repeating to myself, the polyploidies are coming, the polyploidies are coming. Strange, but I like the way it sounds.

The earliest ferns to arrive are the little gold backs. At the first damp they unroll, looking as if they had never left. Even in temporary dry spells they will close, going into a sort of hibernation until it rains again. Then they come out looking as good as before. The maidenhair ferns are the last to appear. They have to be certain the rain is really here before they show themselves. They arrive as tiny green dots on their wiry black stems and slowly enlarge until the dots grow into small ovals. Finally they become delicate greenery, gracing the shadiest, dampest places in the woods. They often grow at the bottom of hills, so they get the last of draining water and persist longer than the earlier-arriving ferns.

Sword ferns are here to enjoy all year. Most wood ferns do the same. Bracken ferns come with spring and depart in early fall. I like and admire them all. I think my favorites remain the gold-back ferns because of their hide-and-seek ways.

After winter rains, the park is fresh and green, trees, banks, rocks, fallen trees and limbs covered with healthy moss. All of the mossy places seem to be sprouting new greenery.

Some interesting things to see in rainy months are mushrooms and other kinds of fungus. The most charming I have seen are little mushrooms I call the parasols. Small, most under four inches tall, with white stems and fragile, pale lavender caps. They come up like little stumps, then unfurl their parasol caps. Before long they start curling their top edges in toward the centers, becoming tiny cups before they shred and disappear. I bought a mushroom book and have consulted several in the library and haven't found any exactly right, though some are similar. The best I can do is think it may be a type of mycena. It remains a lovely little stranger to me.

Growing in the same area are many thin, white, upright fungus. Not surprisingly, these are called finger fungus. Lots of small beige mushrooms appear beside the trails. I have seen pretty white puff balls and impressive coral-like white fungus of some kind. I am not quite sure of what they are called. I simply enjoy trying to identify everything I see in the woods. Generally, I think flowers are easy to know. I find mushrooms difficult.

A broken oak stump is adorned with a climbing assemblage of wide, half-circle shaped beige mushrooms resembling photographs I have seen of oyster mushrooms. Nearby oaks have turkey-tail conks, a type of polypore resembling a turkey tail in full array. Here is another similar but slightly different kind, lined with red. I think it sensible to consider it a red line conk. Growing on other trees and downed limbs are orange, white or brown fungus. I see some mushrooms beginning new growth. These resemble some I saw in a book with a warning to avoid as they are poisonous. I have no trouble obeying that piece of wisdom. I am amused by book descriptions that say something like, "This looks like an edible such and such, but is a deadly poisonous something." That is my attitude toward all wild mushrooms.

The most unusual I see on this fine winter day are three large yellow mushrooms, four to five inches across. They appear to be jelly coated. Imagine large mushrooms slimed with yellow Jell-O. Not something one might want to eat or even touch, but, in their own way, quite beautiful.

I come home from my mushroom walk thinking I have seen unusual, exotic fungus in their home place. The next day I take a stroll through the gardens and grounds where I live and find a shaggy mane mushroom, two puff balls, oyster mushroom like growths on an alder, two kinds of conks, a large handsome mushroom at the base of a redwood by my front window and our very own collection of finger fungus. Sonoma County seems to be a fine source of all things fungus.

Waiting For Rain

Finally a cooler, but sunny day, exactly right for a nice wander in Annadel Park. I cannot drive now, so it is more difficult to get there. My failing eyesight affects many things in my life and one of the more annoying is transport. I only get along because of help from my friends and Oakmont Garden's buses. I ask at the office for golf-cart transport to the park's central entrance, a one and one-half mile walk from here, but it is not available for an hour or so. I decide to enter by another entrance, the polo field and streets of a development called Wild Oak. That is only a walk of one-half mile to reach a park gate.

So, out the door and up the street. I pass the Saturday Farmer's Market, more streets, a church, and start on a path that leads to the place named Wild Oak. I meet walkers and cyclists, both coming and going. We exchange smiles and greetings in our usual way, and I begin to feel at home again.

As I near the end, I pause to read a sticker on the back of a car, something about, "My daughter is an Honor Student," when a woman walked up to me and said, "Are you admiring my license plate?" I had not noticed and looked down to read LAVIGNA. She started telling me about it, how New York Italians might pronounce it, what it might mean, how it might be spelled in Spanish and on and on and on. She expected no answers except smiles and nods, so I did that. She asked if the bikers bothered me. I knew what was coming and replied in the negative.

Those owning and living in Wild Oak want to have bikers banned from their street. They wanted to ban hikers too, but the original county papers and deeds prevented that. They are still trying to oust bicycles. She tells me they frighten her.

I tell her how they have been polite and helpful to me, offering water, assistance, and benches for sitting. We both exaggerate for a while, and I go on my way.

Ah, finally I am in my favorite place. True, I am just walking on the flat, paved Channel Drive, but I am surrounded by fine trees, bushes and plants. The creek is right here by my side, not doing much, only dithering and puddling along. I pass the horse-trailer parking lot and Richardson Trail, leading uphill to all the delights on the hills of Annadel.

I, like the creek, dither along, trying to see everything. I see a low bank where mycena and finger fungus have grown in the past. No, not damp enough yet. Rain is expected tonight, tomorrow and Monday. I think about nice, healing, soothing rain and long for it to heal this too dry forest.

I have been thinking about the gold back ferns lately. We have had a few periods of very light rain. I wonder if this has induced the ferns to start growing. They will open when they have only traces of damp, then, dry again and repeat the freshening the next time it sprinkles. They are hardy, but all that effort diminishes their strength and vitality. So I worry a bit about the state of their health.

I finally spot a few small ones with fronds opened, green and gold bright against the now dry moss where they grow. I keep looking and see quite a few in shady places along the road. The sword and wood ferns have many dry fronds, but are still greenly alive and holding their own where it is shaded and cooler. Bracken ferns are mostly brown and broken with just a few still green. The only polypodies in sight are last winter's withered remnants still hanging on to hillside rocks.

I feel cold and colder as a wintry breeze begins. I wore only a light woolen vest, believing the promise of a sunny day. I hurry along, looking for sun. I see beautiful golden leaves on black oak and big leaf maple trees. The leaves are blowing down, and the wind is stirring those on the ground. I come to the entrance to my favorite trail, North Burma. The nearby creek is dry and dusty where hikers and bikers cross. I look up the creek bed and see nothing but dry, yellowed, shrunken moss and rocks.

I decide to eat my lunch at a table by the ranger station. I remember sitting in the sun there. Alas, I am too late for sun, it is now in the shade of a large live oak. I eat about half my lunch while trying to stretch my feet into sunshine. Not as comfy as I had hoped. I am feeling old, stiff and tired. Since I am all those things, I am not surprised.

I start walking the way I came, pausing to admire, feel, and photograph many wonderfully colorful trees. Some of the oaks have touches of crimson with the yellow and green. I am pleased I am here to see these lovely autumnal changes.

I take a chance, exit at the old waste water plant, call Oakmont Gardens, and soon a golf cart and driver comes tootling down the street to get me. By this time I am resting on some kind of low and sturdy electrical box. It has been about a two mile wander, which is probably my limit these days. I do not think much about tired. I remember the leaves, the ferns and my favorite mossy rocks.

Windy Day

In early April I plan to walk up Spring Creek Trail until I reach the dry creek crossing, but no farther. I do not want to make the climb, up or down, of the precipitous rocks and eroded trail that lie farther up that hill. From the Parktrail entrance and near Spring Creek, the running water sounds are louder than a week ago. There are flowers by the path--purple, yellow, blue, white, and orange. Vigorous lovage plants crowd the hillside with their large leaves and striking flowers.

I enter Annadel Park to see purple-flowered vetch filling the fields along with buttercups. They are joined by blue-eyed grass, each trying to outdo the other in the color contest. The blue is delicate and lovely. The vetch is robust and fills the fields with purple. My vote goes to the buttercups as they are, by far, the happiest.

The underground denizens, gophers and moles, have been at work, leaving freshly churned earth mounds and burrows by the sides of the trails and in the meadows. Woodland ants are surfacing and building small mounds of finely ground dirt.

Spring Creek flows near this trail. The water is milky, gray-white in the deeper pools. The color is given by the mud it has gathered in its course through the hills and down the canyon after the rain.

The hillsides are freshly greened for spring, decorated with bright flowers of many colors. The trunks of the scattered oaks seem dark against the grass and their fresh new leaves flutter in a brisk breeze.

Two women hikers pass by and I hear a snatch of conversation. "He is this big intellectual, a dumpy guy." Conversation always comes in bits and pieces and often leaves me wondering, though I am sometimes relieved I do not have to listen to all of it.

As I go into Spring Creek Canyon, the wind grows stronger and louder. The creek's pleasant murmurings fade under the rushing of wind through the heavy branches of the oaks and bay trees. There are, dimmed by the wind, the noise of high-flying planes. Groaning sounds come from across the creek, a tree or branch rubbing against another.

I walk, searching for trilliums. There were some here last year, but I fail to see any today. The wind is stronger and quite cool. Looking forward to sunshine, I near the dry creek bed. Above here is a Lake Ilsanjo dam. Rocks spill out of the lower part and are tumbled down the way until they reach where the creek flows. This looks as if it may have been the earlier path of Spring Creek. It is a repository for some old logs and rocks of all sizes.

Here is a favorite boulder I use for picnics. It is in shade and too cold and I move my search to the center of the crossing and find a rock of suitable size, shape, and sunshine. It is windier here in the open, so I eat a bit, rest a bit, and start downhill.

In a sunny spot, wild strawberries bloom. A father with two handsome, bright-looking children is coming up the trail. I point out the blooms to the girl and boy and tell them they are strawberries. The father and children indicate interest, and I explain my difficulty with the birds being faster to find the ripe berries than I am. The father says, "We will be faster than the birds." I wish them luck.

I always like to see the small stand of redwoods on this trail and pause to admire them and the quiet, gray-white pools in the creek. I try to stay out of mud on the path as I look for trilliums. No luck with that, so I walk on out, admiring the mission bells as I go, cross the bridge and climb the canyon side of the Vietnam Veteran's Trail. It, too, is quite muddy. I reach a watery place where I have a choice between stepping in mud or in poison oak. It is not a hard choice and I slosh through the puddle.

The white phacelia plants near the top used to fill only one small fence corner, but they have burst out and occupy places on each side of the climb. Over on the lower side they are poking their blossoms out of a rock retaining wall that appears to have been built many years ago.

I stop to rest on a trail bench, take off my jacket and relax in the sun's warmth. The wind lifts again. I replace the jacket and start down the hill. A strong gust of wind takes my hat and I scramble after it. Catching it, I try to clutch the hat with a hand already holding a pole. The lower part of the creek holds water, too, so with a hop, skip and jump, I return to the outside world.

New Leaves

On December 27, 2012 I take my last hike of the year, up to the Vietnam Veteran's Park on the west side of Annadel State Park. It's a foggy day, so there is no view of Santa Rosa or the canyon and hills behind the park. I'm surprised to see catkins on a blue oak and a few small green leaves emerging. I go from tree to tree, look at the tops and see more leaves on the highest branches. On the western side of the hill, the oak trees get lots of sunlight in warm winter weather. That must account for new leaves in December.

On the first Sunday in January, I hike to the top of Richardson Trail on the eastern side of the park to check the oak trees there. As I hike the shady side, I look for new leaves and find none. I reach the top where the trees have much more sun and discover a few. I cannot remember seeing oaks leafing out quite this early.

Later in January, I again climb the Vet's trail. I descend into the canyon behind it and up and down Spring Creek Trail to see a few more leaves on trees that receive a lot of sunlight. I am searching for black oak leaves. When they come, the new leaves will look like soft rose-pink flowers springing out on the bare branches.

In early February, on Channel Drive, I enjoy seeing dainty white milk maid flowers in bloom. I know they will soon have meadow foam as companions. Already the green leaf lace that is part of the charm of meadow foam is growing along the road and paths. The flowering plants will earn their name. They will be lovely foams of ruffled green leaves sprinkled with tiny white blossoms.

Downed oak trees and branches in the park are part of the natural recycling that goes on in the woods. Handsome, striped, rounded fungus grows on some of the decaying wood. It is fairly soft in the early stages and during the rainy season, but as the season progresses it dries and hardens. Some are called conks. I have been told the name refers to a kind of shellfish. I often think if you tap them during the dry season, the sound you hear is conk.

The winter continues to be dry with yellowing moss and dry streambeds. In sunny spots the blue oaks are leafing and buds swell on the branches of black oaks. I continue my oak patrols, looking for new leaves.

Walking down North Burma Trail, I spot three very large white mushrooms. The largest, about eight inches wide, looks handsome, edible and delicious. Knowing nothing about mushrooms, I do not try to harvest them.

In early March, after we have had rains, I see a much larger number of lovage plants than in earlier years. This is another version of the domestic herb of the same name and it, too, has the pleasant fragrance of celery, though it is much stronger in taste.

Near the end, I see a deer standing quietly on the hillside, staring at me. I return the gaze, without moving, and there we are, the two of us, looking, watching, wondering and waiting. She withdraws and I continue, only to soon confront two wild turkeys, a male and a female. The male sounds retreat and off they go, scuttling into the bushes. The usual charming wildlife encounters in the park.

I hike up Richardson Fire Trail on my leaf patrol, seeing more leaves on blue oaks, and flowers and plants with fresh leaves and blooms. At the top, I sit for a bit on the handy bench and admire the lake, meadows and surrounding hills. I continue, passing a meadow with many oak trees, but I am looking into the sun and, though I see some new leaves, I can't see them well. I walk down near the lake, turn and climb up with the sun behind me.

What a sight it is, so many black oaks and all with emerging leaves. The rose-pink colors in their early velvety glow are flower-like and gorgeous. One oak tree grows close

to a dead fir and the branches are entwined, ghostly white remnants of the fir contrasting with the rosy new leaves of the oak. They are of varying heights on the hill, and sometimes stand, festive, beside the grays and greens of other trees, always against the background of fresh green grass and blue sky. Overwhelmed with the beauty of it, almost whirling around in my excitement, I go from tree to tree. No one passing asks what I am seeing, instead discreetly averting their eyes. Asking might involve them in my break with good sense. Some may be thinking about that strange old bird watcher. I am thinking about the trees in the beauty of their new adornments.

Later, trudging down the hill, I know myself fortunate to have this memory for as long as I am able to remember, and a little sad for any who miss so much by not looking up, down and all around.

July Days

On a cool foggy day in early July, I take a short, pleasant stroll on Channel Drive. No hills, no climbing up and down rock-covered trails, only a slow walk to the east end of the drive and return. As I start, there is blue flowered chicory in bloom with a few yellow mustard plants for company. Most fennel plants are now tall, dry stalks topped with clusters of seeds, but across the way in a damp ditch there are still a few late bloomers with fluffs of yellow flowers.

I check the roadside where nightshade plants grow. I am pleased they are thriving and growing larger. Small white flowers, sparkling black berries and bright green leaves make handsome plants. These pretty plants, however, are poisonous.

Just beyond the ranger station there is an aged black oak, with wide, spreading limbs. Lichens and mosses are thick on the tree with a low strand of fishnet lichen reaching more than four feet long. When walking here, I always admire this tree.

Under fir trees the road is littered with pieces of cones. The squirrels don't wait for these seedy treats to ripen. They bite them off the stems, devour the seeds and the leftovers fall. Occasionally they bite a cone off a stem and miss the catch so there are many downed cones and pieces of fir foliage.

I leave the road and go to the last section of Channel Trail where there is a thicket of wild roses and berry vines. Looking closely at the vines, I note a difference in the shape of the leaves and berries. Thinking some of them look like wild raspberries, I sample a flat, rounded berry. It is not quite ripe, but I think it is a raspberry. There are true California blackberries growing here, too.

I reach the end, have a drink from the fountain and start back. Outside the parking area is a dark leaved plum tree loaded with red-purple plums. The other side of the road has blooming mugwort plants. Farther along below the road is one tall cow parsnip in full bloom. The white blossoms stand out near the shadowed creek. In sunny spots there are lots of star thistles and yellow-flowered Klamath weeds. Both invasive non-natives, still the bright yellow of their flowers is cheerful. Some are growing near the red mahogany trunks and pale green leaves of manzanita bushes.

I meet a familiar dog walker. I often see him here with eight or nine leashed dogs. He is cheerful, the dogs well behaved. We exchange greetings. I go on out, having enjoyed my slow walk, looking, listening and learning.

Two days later I start up W.R. Richardson fire trail, soon switching to Steve's S Trail. It is quite steep, but pleasant, as it is not as worn as most trails here. It climbs with many twists and turns and lots of lovely vistas to admire.

My walk began on a cool, cloudy morning, and now I see blue openings among the clouds with shafts of sunlight breaking through, illuminating the fern-covered hillside. Everything is looking fresh and new. Blue sky, deep-green fir trees above, and many California bay laurel trees, their leaves gleaming in the fresh sunshine. I look up through oaks' mossed branches. The undersides look dark, almost black. The sunshine above gives a golden glow to the mossy branch edges. It is so lovely I pause to admire the difference. The hillside, both above and below, is green with ferns.

Fallen trees lie where they fell in earlier years. I remember hiking up here in winter about three years ago and, finding a downed tree across the trail, chose to climb up and over it rather than retracing my steps. Soon an open gateway had been cut, with tree lengths on both sides and the cut log rolled out of the way.

I finish Steve's Trail and re-enter Richardson to resume my hike toward Lake Ilsanjo and look ahead where, against the blue sky, I see a group of tall, dead firs, broken and gray black, surrounded by shorter green trees. Dead firs are found throughout the park. I have been told when the land became parkland, the firs, undesirable in the oak forest, were girdled to prevent their shading out the young oaks. It seems as if most of those trees still stand, now blackened with broken gray limbs, but too tough to give up and fall. I often wish they had tried to eradicate the Himalayan blackberries.

I reach the top, look down at the sparkling blue lake, and wonder if I want to walk all the way down. I go toward the lake and, when almost there, decide to turn back. I climb up the hill and, seeing the entrance to South Burma Trail, decide to try a bit of this trail, described to me as steep, rocky and rutted. It is good in the beginning, covered with flat, dried mud, but becomes increasingly narrow, crowded by vegetation. There is a lone, blue self-heal flower and some pretty fleabane coming into bloom. Many varieties of fleabane have been used in the past as strewing herbs. Cottages and castles alike used these because when fleabane arrived, bugs departed, or so it was said.

After enjoying the flowers, I return to the pleasantly wide Richardson trail. Down the way, there is a mother turkey with three gawky, adolescent offspring. Turkey mother and children wander off across the meadow to take refuge in some coyote bushes. Near the trail is a clump of rose bushes and standing alone is one perfect, small pink rose, a lovely change from the dry grass behind it.

I return to the bottom of Richardson trail and have walked more than four miles, am increasingly tired, now ready to sit and rest, but must continue to my car.

A ranger driving by with a passenger, an older woman, stops his truck. They are looking for her runaway dog. I haven't seen it and tell him about the remains of a campfire I saw on Cobblestone Trail last month. He hadn't known about that one.

A woman's voice starts shouting, "Here doggy, here nice doggy." A dog barks. The ranger calls, "We are looking for a dog." The voice yells, "He's here. Here, nice doggy, nice doggy, come here, doggy." The ranger gets out of the truck and starts to walk. The lost dog woman looks pleased but anxious. The dog shouting woman continues to shout, the dog to bark. The ranger disappears into the shrubbery. Tired, but smiling at this unfolding mini-drama, I depart.

How Dry It Is

In early June I walk up a dry, dusty Richardson Trail. What had been thick green moss on the rocks in the seasonal stream bed is now fading, shrunken and yellowed. The grass is dry, pale and brittle, many pods are open and the seeds have fallen. The exceptions are most burr chervil plants, still a bit green and clutching those bristly seeds that will later be clinging to any hiker unlucky enough to brush against them.

I notice the wild roses seem to have stopped blooming. The bushes have many hips, but not a rose remains. I see tiny spots of pink on the ground, the prolific and tough red-stemmed fillarees, and all of them seem to be so water deprived they are only an inch or two tall. There are yellow dandelion-like flowers of various heights flowering, false dandelion or hawk's beard. The plentiful yellow Klamath weeds are still blooming, though most are fading with browning blossoms.

I saw a family with two small girls and a baby in a stroller in the parking lot. In the back of the stroller was a paper bag filled with those invasive yellow weeds. Flowers in the parks should not be picked, but I won't miss those pesky Klamath weeds.

Later in the month, after an illness and staying in for a time, I need to go for a short walk. I want to see if the small but formidable Fitch's spike-weeds growing on the Lake Trail to Annadel have commenced blooming. In the trailside dryness there are quite a few yellow trefoils and, surprisingly, a few pink fillarees are still holding on. Fragile toughness. Finally, after looking at a lot of spiky plants, I see a few of Fitch's pets beginning their bloom. The yellow daisy flowers are not quite opened, but soon they will be looking rather pretty, just don't touch. More yellow is by the trail in the bright color of Russian thistles.

There is a memorable live oak near this path. I stop, admire and take a picture. My picture-taking ability is not enough to portray the magnificence of this large tree. It must be very old, a grandfather among oaks. Nearby is another smaller tree with poison oak vines climbing high through the branches. Some of the vine leaves are turning an autumnal red. I feel it is too soon.

I don't go far, turning back at the bridge leading hikers to Rough Go and other park trails. As I walk back, I admire the color of the dry grass along the trail and hills. Almost all the grasses are blonde and dancing along with this morning's soft breeze. The seeds have fallen and the lightened plants are having a time in the sun. The Canary grasses, still loaded with seeds, stand heavily, waiting their time to join this short celebration. The teasels are amazing, stiffly tall and decorated with fringes of tiny white blossoms and crowns of small, sharply pointed green leaves.

I am used to seeing them with their late summer look... dry, prickly, ready to stab any finger.

In a few days, I have a short, pleasant saunter along Channel Trail. The morning is refreshingly cool with clouds and sun, alternately blue sky and grey. I start at the horse trailer parking lot in rather dense shade and encounter a flock of turkeys on their way up a hill. I wait for them and notice a dead log with four interesting fungus attached. They are hard shelled, white and puffed, reminding of puff balls, though with flattened, elongated shapes. Three have been broken, one of them shattered, and they seem to be a like puff balls. Like those, when dry and hard, if broken a spray of brown spores puffs out scattering everywhere in the vicinity. Interested and curious, I snap a picture and go on to look for new puzzles.

The grass-covered hills above the path are dry; the remaining splashes of green are mostly poison oak with some creeping snowberry bushes and a lesser number of woodland pea vines.

In a small draw above the path a female deer stands, watching me closely, sniffing for my scent. I stop and return her stare, then she relaxes, shakes her head and, reassured by my stillness, scratches behind an ear with a hoof. She frisks her tail and ears to ward off flies as she nibbles the leaves of bushes and goes up the hill with me following on the trail. Gradually, the distance between us widens and she disappears into the trees.

Here, among fir trees, the shade is dense and some maidenhair ferns are still green, though the goldback ferns are closed. Wood and sword ferns seem well, as do many small green plants. As I enter the province of sun-loving oaks, the summer changes are advancing. A winter creek crossing is now deep in dust and some fern fronds are drooping and dry. I am surprised by one Ithuriel's spear doggedly holding a few flowers. It is partially withered, but still has four, deeply blue flowers brightening the trailside. Suddenly, six wild turkeys come out of some bushes, strut across the trail, go to the road below and promenade down to the creek.

On a bank having many Indian warrior plants, a few remain green, fluffy and fern like, surprising against so many other dry plants. As usual, I stop to see some hazelnut bushes, and I wonder at the white mottled appearance of some leaves. The white spots look like mildew. It seems unusual in this dry season. I notice the conk fungus on logs is becoming hard and lighter in color as it does every summer.

Yesterday was the first day of summer and I see it here. The slim Solomon's seal plants are far gone in dryness. Oakmont pond is evaporating, growing dark and dense. The blackberry blossoms are few and the berries are ripening. As I think of summer, the clouds recede, the sun brightens, and the day begins to warm.

Wandering in the Rain

I knew today's walk would be a short, quick outing, but I needed to be outside and moving. Before I left, I checked with weather.com. I asked for an hourly report and learned the morning is cloudy and cool with no rain expected until one or two in the afternoon.

On this cloudy March day, I am in Annadel by eleven, ready to go. I decide to confine this short wander to Channel Drive as everywhere else is rather muddy. My favorite seasonal creek is having a pleasant run today, nothing elaborate, but adequate. The larger creek below looks like last week. It has not received enough new water to be excited.

I admire the vigorously green growing poison oak. That is all the friendship I am willing to offer. Thinking it is a terrible pest that nothing short of world domination will satisfy, I keep my distance from this Putin of the plant world. Here and there are more bright buttercups, cheery against the new green of poison oak.

Pausing to reach for and feel the soft fuzziness of hazelnut leaves, I am careful not to pick or bruise them as I just want to feel their well-remembered softness. Even though we have had only a little rain, the moss and ferns reflect the damp. The moss is a more luxuriant green and the ferns have increased in size and number. Everything is damply renewed. If I were a frog, I would be croaking in pleasure. Lacking their song, I just go along, admiring it all.

Every time I come here, I look carefully for a long-time favorite, the little pink star flower. I see lots of the star-shaped leaves, but it is too early for the flowers. When I was a little girl, living in redwood country, I called them fairy flowers.

In an open place by the road there are myriad small

white blooms, meadow foam, milk maid, miner's lettuce, and chickweed. Something new has been added, a small white flower named shepherd's purse for its bag-shaped seed pods. To my pleasure I see three flowering plants called red henbit. Why or where they received this name, I have no idea.

Snowberry plants are flourishing all over the place, both the bush and the creeping variety. There are sprinkles of water on their leaves, glittering like dots of ice. A little sunlight turns the water into sparkling flowers.

I stop by the Indian Warrior's bank to admire their blossoms. It appears there are fewer plants than last year. The air is now cooler and damper, so I turn back and, as always, admire the blue of hound's tongue blooms. Not a lovely name for such fine flowers, but it reflects the shape of the plant leaves.

I notice pretty white blooms on the wild strawberry plants. They look healthy. In a damper place, I see creeping buttercups. These small plants like lots of water and frequently grow by the side of roads where there is runoff. They have fewer petals and are much shorter than the California buttercups, but the flower's shape and color are unmistakably buttercup.

A cyclist goes by and gives a friendly grin. I nod and smile back. His is a familiar face, as I have been seeing him in here for some time. He always has a smile, as if he is happy to see me, coming back, time after time. I, too, am glad to be back and see that pleasant smile.

I feel a few light raindrops. The tree canopy lessens and the watery spray increases. I pull a scarf over my head and hurry my wander to a serious walk. I look ahead, hoping to stay under trees, but that is not going to be possible, so I just enjoy the rain as I go. I stop to see fresh white flower spikes on some slim Solomon's seal plants.

As I drive out, I pause by the Annadel Park sign to look for the sun cups that return here every spring. These are short, sunny yellow flowers whose name describes them. To my pleasure, there are several flowering near the sign and many plants not yet in bloom. They are generously accompanied by tall buttercups and the creeping variety, too. An all-over sprinkle of pink flowered fillaree plants bloom in every available spot. It is spring, indeed it is

I feel as if my outdoor time has been too brief, and I go to Spring Lake to see how it looks in the rain. I park where I can see the water. After I am comfortably settled for some entertaining water watching, the rain stops. I sit quietly, as does the lake, scarcely a ripple. It is a pleasant interlude and I take time to enjoy it.

Inventory

It is time to look at the oak trees on the west side of Annadel Park as some may have new leaves. I walk up the Vietnam Veteran's Trail in mid-February and see a few blue oaks with the beginnings of spring leaves. There are none of the many wildflowers that will be here later. Some buckeye trees are fully leafed, others are just starting. Their first leaf shoots remind me of endive. Since the large seeds of these trees are somewhat poisonous, I do not think I will be adding their leaves to my dining.

I decide to walk down the back part of this trail to Spring Creek Canyon below. It is steep, but always interesting. At the start there are lots of phacelia plants. I have been watching these for the past three years and like to see them spreading. Soon the tightly curled white flowers with fernlike leaves will be blooming among the dark rocks. A flower book says they prefer growing in rocky areas and I think, my dear phacelias, you have picked the right place. I carefully go down this rocky hill, watching for loose rocks and mud in the trail, stopping from time to time, checking trees for change and the ground for new plants. There are new beginnings of many things and, best today, a few blooming white milk maids.

The water in Spring Creek is diminished. Running last week, it is now trickling, dribbling and disappearing underground to reappear a bit farther down the way. It has many small pools to which mud has given a milky tint. It looks pretty, though in need of refreshing.

I am at the start of Canyon Trail, but decide to go up Spring Creek a short distance. I want to see the mission bell plants whose home is around the corner. I visit them often. Here they are, fresh, green and healthy.

69

Going back on the wide fire trail I notice more of the charming milk maid flowers. Nearby is a place, where in watery times, frogs live. When passing, I always slow a bit to hear their unobtrusive croaking. No bullfrog sounds, just a little springtime singing. I pass lots of young lovage plants, two vines of wild cucumber and the beginnings of many buttercups. This has been a pleasant way to spend a couple of sunny hours.

Continuing my own short survey of plants in Annadel Park, I take more hikes in the next few days. There is a group of manzanitas near the entrance to North Burma Trail that have been blooming for some time. The spent blossoms are falling with an intensity varying from a light snowfall to a heavy storm. The ground under one small tree is white with tiny, bell-shaped flowers.

I walk up to the creek crossing where the trail is quite muddy. I see I could cross with a bit of splashing, but there is more mud on the other side. I decide to go downhill and take pictures of the stream. It is looking happy today, low but cheerful, with glints of light. It ripples and gurgles as it wanders down among mossy rocks. Here and there, semi-opened buckeye leaves bend near the stream, sunlight on them, making memorable spring presentations.

The next day, I decide Richardson Trail needs me to review its progress toward spring. There are a few more white milk maids and, to my pleasure, I see a pale pink one. I have seen these before, but not often.

Goldback ferns have returned, but most have a large number of spent, browned fronds. Now these plants are growing new leaves. The early starts look like tiny, almost white fungus, round and fragile, by the roots of the fern. Their black stems grow and gradually begin unfolding the tightly closed fronds. Finally, after this winter's off and slightly on again rains, these ferns are renewing themselves.

Here is a small, open, grass-covered field, half-circled by tall fir trees. On the edge of the firs facing the trail is a black oak, trying to leaf, low growing, leaning toward morning and sunlight before it is blocked each day by the fir's heavy afternoon shade. On the opposite hill, these oaks, open to morning and afternoon sun, are in bloom, almost fully leafed, though some of the rosy spring glow remains on the leaves and tassels.

Shortly after I make the last turn to go to the top of the hill, I look to the right where there are always white camas lilies in springtime. To my surprise many are already budded as are some on the other side of the trail. This is a damp place: the grass is greener and taller and water still stands in a small drainage ditch. I must return soon as they may be blooming .

Reaching the top I am quite tired, being out of practice,

and decide not to go down to the lake. That little extra would turn this four-mile hike into a five-mile one. I walk a bit farther as I want to see a meadow that holds camas lilies and black oak trees. I see fewer lily plants, not the amount I remember from previous years.

While walking, I remember the flowers I have seen at earlier times. Since it is almost spring, I look to see if the plants have returned. I am thrilled when I see, in the expected places, four hound's tongue plants, two with buds. Nearby, starting to grow, are new leaves of shooting stars and buttercups. Wondering about the lesser amounts of camas lilies, I am relieved to see some things remain constant.

As a very tired me trudges down this hill, I forget the fatigue by remembering at the proper places the Johnny Jump-Ups I saw here last year, the Calypso orchids under redwoods over there and at this meadow, all those lovely wild roses. After renewing my brief acquaintance with the pink milk maid, I reluctantly leave this garden.

Hiking Through a Cluttered Mind

Why do I hike instead of taking short walks around the neighborhood? It would be more suitable at my age to walk. One reason is because it is quiet and pleasant on the trails. With so much to see and experience there, it is a fine time to think about anything and everything. I also find plants and trees that are new to me, and I renew my enjoyment of ones I have known since childhood.

Hard and difficult trails are a challenge. I want to try them. I walk slowly because of age, but it gives me opportunities to observe. I walk alone because I do not know anyone who wants to do this. I see young people rushing along, enjoying the exercise and hope they slow down to see the beauty and wonder of their surroundings. I am grateful age has brought the ability to learn from and enjoy everything I see.

I recall a recent November hike: where I went, what I did, and what I thought while hiking. Sometimes recollections of thoughts on these walks are hikes through my cluttered mind. Here is the hike and some of the thoughts.

I go into Annadel Park and start walking up Richardson Trail, steep but easy, switching to Steve's S trail, because, though steeper, it cuts a mile off the trip to the top. As always, when I walk, I must slowly adjust my breathing. The steeper the trail, the longer it takes to stop my asthmatic wheezing and breathe normally.

I start up the stairs that mark the entry and see lots of fresh green moss, revived by the recent rains. Steve's Trail goes through a forest of fir trees. The ground is beautifully covered with California wood and sword ferns. One fast hiker passes me and hurries up the path. I think, look at her go, but she is young, and I see no other hikers on Steve's Trail today.

I use my hiking poles as I climb. The trail is littered with small pieces of black obsidian, so many that the ground glistens. I remember Lake County and the obsidian thrown out by the volcano, Mt. Konocti. My book on Bay Area geology tells about Sonoma volcanics, but is not more specific as to place. The explosions here were millions of years ago

I see a small yerba buena plant. It is the first one I have

seen up here, though I find many on lower trails. It is in the mint family, wonderfully fragrant, named the good herb by the Spanish, and long used for its medicinal properties by Indians. Later discovered by American settlers, it is still valued by herbalists. I cannot resist taking just one leaf, rubbing it between my fingers and inhaling the healing fragrance because it is marvelously refreshing. The trail meanders, has switchbacks, and dips in a low place where a creek runs in winter. Results of the rain show on the trail. Fir needles, bay leaves and various kinds of forest duff display patterns of recently flowing water

Nearing the top I come to places where the beautiful white camas, or zygadene lilies, bloom in spring. I think of Lewis and Clark who, during that winter at Fort Clatsop, when game was scarce, relied on blue camass bulbs, baked in campfire coals. I wonder how, in the winter, they would know which kinds were safe, as the blue is edible and the white, poisonous. Of course, they traded with Indians for them and Indians knew where to get the right kind. I remember the trip my husband and I took so many years ago to the East and then West to follow Lewis and Clark's trail to the Pacific

I look at wild rose bushes under the forest canopy, wondering if these are wood roses. I know those growing in the sun farther down the trail are California wild roses. These leaves are a bit different. I peer at them, looking for rose hips, but no luck. The hips have different shapes on the two varieties, the wood rose being rounder.

Arriving at Richardson, I go to the top where there is a bench and a view of Lake Ilsanjo, and sit for a few minutes to enjoy the view. I wonder about how few acorns I have seen this year. When we were children, my father told us the Indians used to say a heavy crop meant a bad winter. A light crop indicated better weather. Last year there were many acorns and lots of rain

I admire again, as many times before, the handsome black or Oregon oaks growing up here. I especially like these oak trees for the beauty of their velvety pink leaves in spring and autumn colors. In the fall they are the first oak leaves to drop. I pass the entrance to South Burma Trail and start down to Lake Trail, where there is a group of teen runners and bikers exchanging laughs. The runners continue down Richardson, and the bikers start down South Burma Trail, which appears to have recently been closed with a barrier and tape, now moved.

Walking on down Richardson Trail toward the lake, I realize before I reach it I'm not up for it today and start back. I decide to return all the way on this trail; though it is longer, it is not as steep as Steve's S. A good reason to choose this one is because there are people still walking and biking on it as the day grows late

There is loose rock going downhill, so I use my poles with care and watch where I step. Whenever I see a bench, I pause and have some water. I try to pace myself, which is easy to do on this trail. Here is a bench where hikers often sit to look at the view, and I stop there. Farther down on my right is a long tumble of moss-covered boulders where a creek runs in winter. Today has not been difficult and less than four miles. It was another pleasant day in the park with lots of not so heavy thinking and nature all over the place.

Flashes of Fall

In late September some leaves are falling, lingering in the cool morning air as they wander toward the ground. They seem to regret leaving their tree and gently settle to earth, on it, but not yet part of it.

Coming up from a tangled mass of blackberry bushes, grows one tall branch of an elderberry. Topping it is a large cluster of ripe elderberries. The balance of the bush is consumed by blackberry brambles.

I start up Richardson Trail, but soon climb the wooden stairs that lead to Steve's S Trail. The "S" is said to be for secret. I think it stands for steep.

The sun is beginning to show through the overhead branches, and the dark forest starts to come to life. I look below and see a few large leaves of a maple, now yellow, turned to a glowing gold as the sun shines through them. On the opposite hill, mist lingers in the tall trees. Only the tops are touched by sunlight.

The trail is in good shape, the lighter traffic reflected in the relative lack of wear. The ground here seems to be graveled with black, glassy chips of obsidian. Tree roots are exposed, some shiny with wear, others dark and battered. They persist, attached to healthy, large trees, so the wear doesn't seem to have been an inhibiting factor.

Numerous small, shiny-leaved Oregon grape plants grow under the big firs. On the bank above me, sword and wood ferns are well in spite of the dryness. There are pale stalks of departed sweet cicely and brown, crumpled remains of some ferns.

I like this trail, but today my time is limited and I turn back before the end. While going down, I notice moss growing over much of the ground. Trees have yellowed, shrinking in on themselves, and becoming thinner as the dry season continues. Along the path are spread long, flat, shrunken, now white leaves of Indian soap plants. In spring and summer this tall plant with pointed leaves and spikes of white evening blooming flowers are everywhere; now, just the dry weathered leaves remain.

When I return to the horse trough area, I sit to rest. I hear the sound of a biker coming down Richardson Trail, fast and can't see him yet, but wonder if he will be able to stop. He races down and slides sideways into the gate with a loud clang. He casts a glance toward me. Could that be a slight look of embarrassment? I am glad to see he is all right. He gives a laugh, then calls to a friend still riding down.

I decide to hike Channel Trail. I have never seen the trail so dusty and worn. There is a section where the thick dust is almost white in color and finely powdered. It covers a short, steep climb. I consider what a heavy winter rain will do to this bank. I imagine the deep layer of dust washed away and wonder how much of the earth underneath will remain.

The path leads back to Channel Drive, where I find a friendly boulder and sit down for an apple and some water. While resting, I look at a nearby rock bank, fern covered last spring, now brown and dry except for a few final tendrils of green honeysuckle vines curling down from the top. A small, bright green big leaf maple is trying to grow in the rock, brightening the bottom.

Returning to the trail, I go up again and find yerba buena plants surviving in the shade. Farther along, I am delighted to find galium still growing in some profusion. I have seen it here for several years and been happy to see it each time. In my gardens, I grew a relative, galium odoratum or sweet woodruff, a fragrant, pretty, shade-loving plant. The one I see here is trifolum. It has a close relative, aparine, also known as cleavers. A fast- growing pest, it will truly cleave to almost anything. Unfortunately, it grows profusely in forests. When dried, the odoratum variety has a fine vanilla odor. In medieval times, this fragrant herb, called Our Ladies Bedstraw, was used to stuff mattresses and was strewn on floors. Teutonic warriors were said to go into battle with a sprig in their helmets, as it gave courage and good luck. It is still used as an ingredient in German May Wine. The fragrance of the plants brings to me memories of past gardens, and May wine garden parties.

Today is about the return of fall, and I think of all the dark rainy days between now and the return of spring flowers.

March Wandering

A March walk can start in sunshine and soon turn cold and windy. When this happens, I look for a sunnier place. As I start toward Spring Creek and Canyon trails, I decide to seek the sun, turn back, and walk toward Spring Lake. Near the entry to Rough Go Trail, the bank contains large slabs of dark rock. Among the rocks are many blooming blue dick plants. What a sight these delicate, light-blue blossoms are against the dark, looming wall.

For a change I take the horse trail on the east side of Spring Creek. Seeing a fine boulder of just the right size and roundness, I sit down on it and turn my back to the view of Santa Rosa to face a meadow above the trail. When walking here, I often stop to look at the large boulders scattered about the fields. The shapes of the dark, lichen-patterned rock always remind me of a herd of cows lying down after a meal to ruminate, contemplate, or whatever cows do while resting.

On St. Patrick's Day, I hike up Canyon Trail just far enough, but not too far. The trail sides are alight with flowers, blue, yellow, white and pink. I think it is a lovely day to be out and wandering. In a far corner is a gathering of smaller rocks, closer together, reminding me of a huddle of sheep.

I am admiring a flower-enhanced hillside when a gentleman passes. He asks, "Do you know about flowers?" Pointing at a flower, he adds, "Here is a pink comet."

"As a child growing up in California, we always called them shooting stars."

"Quite right, I was thinking of England."

"In universal plant language, as you know, I think it may be called dodecatheon."

"You do know your flowers. Have a great day flower viewing." I wish him a great hike and a good day.

I continue up the hill thinking I will stop soon, but wanting to see the next or the after the next thing, so on I go. I lunch at the picnic table by Marsh Trail and stop to admire the woodwardia ferns by the horse trough. I continue, soon arriving at a sad place of many dead and dying madrone trees. These trees look worse each year and I wonder about the cause.

A few quail run about near a small outlet that drains from the lake. A little boy runs up and starts calling to them. The shouting causes the quail to scatter under bushes. I can't tell if he is trying to call them or frighten them, and don't think he knows either.

At Lake Ilsanjo, I realize it is time to turn back. A ranger stops his truck to talk for a short time. We discuss our good fortune to be in this splendid place at this lovely time of year. He goes to inspect a dam and I start down the hill. By the time I am out, I have had six hours of wandering, a fine time and feel more than a little tired.

Later in the month, I start my walk at the Parktrail entrance, and go on the path leading into Annadel Park. The many bright buttercups growing and blooming on both sides of the trail make the cool morning feel warmer. I plan to wander a bit, but keep it easy, no really steep places.

I go up Canyon Trail where flowers bloom in profusion. All the usual beauties are here, and what a lovely sight they are. Standing by a bank admiring the flowers, I notice small bits of lavender with pink. I step into the ditch to get a closer look, and lean down to try to identify these tiny blossoms. It looks like, can it be? Yes, it is seldom-seen blue-eyed Mary. I look up and around the hill above this bank. Little seldom-seen is all over the place and has been transformed into often-seen-blue-eyed Mary.

Happy at my luck in seeing so many flowers, I return downhill and enter Spring Creek Trail for another short stroll. I stop at a place where mission bells grow, and am delighted to see they are already in bloom. Their exotic green and brown flowers are always a pleasure, so I stay to admire them for a time.

Continuing to a sunny clearing, there is a log the right size for sitting. It has no poison oak, brush or tall grass close by, so it looks good. I pound it with my walking sticks. There

are no answering rattles and I sit down. I always do this when preparing to rest on logs or rocks. Rattlesnakes do not like to be around people and, if disturbed, will usually warn you away.

As always, stopping at the restful bench by Canyon Bridge, I notice several thriving California fuschia plants growing nearby, and think of how handsome their red flowers will be later this year. From this place there are good views of trees and hills, and I sit in peaceful admiration. A woman with hiking poles comes down from Spring Creek and, answering to my smile says, "Another great day in paradise." I agree and leave to climb up the canyon side of the Vietnam Veteran's trail.

It is narrow, steep, rock-filled and, in places, muddy. A beautiful place to be. Views into the canyon below, mossy rocks by quiet pools, many trees, blooming bushes, plants and flowers make it a short, easy walk. I enjoy it so much I forget it can be a bit difficult.

The little white foam flowers are spreading on the hill, and a tiny pink flower, linanthus, has joined in brightening the trail edges. At the top there are plants of white phacelia in bloom.

I find a bench with a nice view of Santa Rosa, and sit down to enjoy. I see a gorgeous flowering crabapple tree beside a house down the hill. The sky has become cloudy, and the wind grows cooler. I stay for a bit, realize it is time to retreat. and wander on down the hill and out.

Fading Fast

As I walked in Annadel during May, I saw how rapidly spring flowers have come and gone in this dry year. I have the feeling, if I am not here the day a flower blooms, I will not see it as it will fade the next. I walked through a favorite flower place on Channel Trail in the middle of the month and found most flowers had gone. Two tiny wine cup clarkias remained, looking sad and lonely. In other years at this time, there have been many more clarkias of different varieties.

Back to Annadel and up Richardson Trail on a later walk, large ferns are still looking good, though the small polypodies and gold backs are fading. There were a few flowers blooming; not at all the profusion usually found here at this time.

On the first day of the Memorial Day Holiday, I hike up Richardson Trail and find the grass drying, with flowers and ferns looking like the end of June. In the damper places, a few flowers remain bright. The little fairy lanterns are showing their yellow light, though petals are fading, some dropping as their unusual seed pods develop. I see one lone blue-eyed grass flower, the last in a cluster of blade-like leaves. There is a very late blooming white foam flower sheltering under an old piece of log.

I am surprised to see fewer people here than expected on this sunny Saturday, then think it may be a bit too sunny, as the weather is predicted to be unusually warm this weekend. An occasional biker races down the dry fire trail, raising a dust cloud large enough to cause the hikers, me too, to turn our backs and cover our eyes as the dust envelops us.

Woodland pea vines are looking green and healthy with their perky pink blooms. A bench, where I like to sit and admire the view, is in too much sun this morning, and I keep walking. The open meadows are dry, already colored beige. I stop to admire and smell a large collection of Yerba Buena plants under a fir tree. The fragrance of the leaves is as deliciously good as expected.

Reaching a shaded bench, I have a rest, some water, and am ready to go. The best refresher is looking uphill at the heavily shaded portion of the trail, as it goes through firs and redwoods on its way to Lake Ilsanjo.

The hillside is covered with sword and wood ferns still looking good. This part of the hill has large trees with dense shade, and ferns thrive. Many touches of pink are scattered throughout the hillsides, all of it provided by more woodland pea vines. I am surprised to see how many are still blooming, and so cheerful they make me smile. The little ground-cover plants, such as gallium, also seem happy and well. Some are starting to show the creamy color of their minute blossoms.

This is a steep hill and, in spite of the shade, I feel the

temperature rising. I reach a picnic table, have a drink ,and consider whether to go up or down. I had planned to go to the lake today. I think it is too hot and decide to go back so I can be out by noon.

As I begin, a young woman passes me, stops, turns back and asks, "Where does this trail go?" I answer, "You are headed down to the parking lot." "Oh, no!" She exclaims. "I want to go to North Burma Trail. I just came up Steve's Trail and I thought this took me to it." "You only have to turn around and go the opposite way," I tell her. I give her directions, and we talk of the park, the trails, the rocks and plants, how much she is starting to like this park, and I say it is an important part of my life. We part with good wishes, she to continue her long hike, and I to go downhill.

The last section of the downhill trek is more in sunshine than in shadow and, as always, when the day is hot, I cross back and forth to stay in the shade. Sometimes it is all in sun, and I walk faster there, then I dawdle along under the cover of trees. No matter how warm, I always slow to admire the fine new blooms on the wild rose bushes. Occasionally, a blue Ithuriel's spear shows in the drying grass and, very seldom, a pink clarkia in flower.

The heat is increasing near the end of the trail and I, too, am fading fast.

Colors of Spring

During pauses in early March's rain showers, I enjoy some short walks, taking one brief wander on paved Channel Drive to avoid the large puddles and mud on the trails. The nearby creek is making pleasant, happy sounds. At last, this creek has some water to work with. No longer muttering at its' lack, now it seems to say, "With all this water I'm off to run with the river and on to the end."

As I walk the flat, safe drive I see the hiker's friend, poison oak, coming to life all along the edges. The vine presents itself in its most alluring colors. In shade, bright flashes of fiery red show in the new sprouts. In sun the leaves are in soft greens and pinks, appearing as the prettiest, friendliest plant in the forest.

Here is a handsome bank, sometimes graced with ferns and flowers. Now it is rich with ferns, moss, newly opened leaves of snow berries and cream bushes, and outbreaks of damply lush lichen. I slow, stop and look at new and old growth, and see the spring's first bloom of an Indian warrior. Delighted, I enjoy the red beauty and take its picture.

It starts to sprinkle, and I hurry to my car. On the way, I see two yellow mushrooms, but this is not a good time for fungus admiration, and I don't stop.

A few days later, I return, parking near North Burma Creek that is sparkling in the sunshine, its green moss glowing. I smell the fragrance of the nearby oso berry blooms, now covering those bushes with little white flowers. A bit farther along, I see my first hound's tongue flower of the year. It looks pink with a slight shade of lavender. Perhaps it will darken to the usual brilliant blue. I walk on to see if the Indian warrior flower is well. I am pleased to see it is splendid, and the red color has spread. I see a second Indian Warrior growing among the ferns on the bank. All of the ferns seem taller and healthier.

I find one small, blooming mission bell. I am happy to see this charming yellow-green, brown-spotted lily. There are not a lot of these, and the coloring makes them a bit hard to see, mixed as they are with other green plants growing on the dark forest floor.

Later I walk into Annadel on the Spring Lake fire trail. The sky is blue, the sun is shining, the grass looks healthier, and Spring Creek has water running in it. Crossing the bridge, I turn into the park and look at the rock bank on my left for the blue dick flowers growing here every year. I soon see them, perhaps smaller than their usual size, but blue and beautiful. This drought year may have lessened their size, but not their will to bloom. The high rock bank has some water dripping through the broken, tumbled layers of basaltic rocks, adding to the mud and puddles on the trail.

The trail has a high bank on the left, with a steep hill above. The bank holds large rocks with lateral breaks, embedded in red volcanic soil. As you walk toward Annadel, the rocks give way to broken, aged lava, and soil interspersed with areas of conglomerate-like pieces of rock embedded in decomposing lava. As you progress, there are fewer pieces of rock, more lava and soil until, finally, the bank consists mainly of red-brown volcanic soil. I always enjoy this section of rock, lava and soil. Its appearance and composition fascinates me. I stop, look, and wonder about earth movements and such. It must appear to be another of my crazy old woman moments. Perhaps a passerby thinks, there she is again. This time she is staring at dirt. Strange.

Near the Annadel Park sign, I see the soft pink color of

new leaves of black oaks. The creek is making water sounds and white milk maid flowers bloom in the green grass. What a joy it all is. What a fine day. What a lucky person I am! Then, I see a bit of yellow, no, two, no, many buttercups. Spring is here. It rained yesterday, it may be colder and cloudy tomorrow, but today there is no denying, this is spring. I must restrain my inclination to go lie down among the buttercups. I might squash one little yellow beauty.

The next day is warm but looks like rain will arrive at any time, so I take a quick climb up the Vietnam Veteran's Trail on the western side of Annadel Park. I never need an

excuse for an outing, but do think I need to see the phacelia flowers growing here. It may be too early for the curled white flowers, but perhaps they will surprise me.

This is a rock-filled trail, though a short one. As usual, the blue oaks are leafing with no undue display, light green leaves and inconspicuous blooms. Not so, the flowers blooming below. Sunny buttercups, bright blue dicks, wisps of purple vetch, and here and there, spreads of fiery orange California poppies. Even the miner's lettuce is sprouting early white flowers on this west-facing hill.

I go to see my friends, the phacelias, and find the plants taller and healthy, but there are no early flowers. I climb a bit higher, hoping to see fiddlenecks, and see two of the unusual little flowers. These early bloomers are small, each having only one bright orange flower. They have not yet reached a size where more flowers will cause them to curl downward in the shape of a violin neck. Still, there's no mistaking it: they are making sunny spring music accompanied by a lovely chorus of the many colored blossoms shining in the green grass and gray rocks.

Canyon Spring

In April, I walk into Annadel Park by way of the Vietnam Veteran's Park entrance. The many tall lovage plants are laden with seeds, making good forage for birds and small animals. I am delighted to see a springtime display by the resident Virgin's Bower, a kind of clematis, which is climbing a bay tree. A large man and a woman overtake me. He stops and, with a pleased look, announces, "I saw a mountain lion right down there last week. Same time as now, about ten in the morning." A gleam in his eyes made me think he hoped I would be frightened. I smile, "Ah, yes, I saw one last year, just across the creek."

As soon as I go over the bridge to Canyon Trail, I am greeted by numerous small, pink plectritis flowers and a cream bush in bud. There are lots of little white fluff flowers. The name says it all, a piece of fluff with fuzzy stem and leaves. There are many ookows with twisted stems and pretty blue flowers. I remember baby books with pictures of "moo cows." I restrain a very old impulse to demonstrate by saying moo, moo. I doubt ookows care, but am not sure about hikers.

This area has soil of decomposed sandstone and, though the flowers are many, they are small because the soil is poor. Some of the dirt is very fine, like dust. Most look like beach sand, and in other places it's quite coarse and pebbly. The trailside banks and hills have interesting exposures of various kinds and colors of sandstone. I keep telling myself, remember, when you're admiring the rocks, watch where you put your feet on them. So I proceed carefully, walk three steps, pause, admire the scenery, then three more steps. Works for me.

In years of ordinary rainfall, there is a small stream here, making its way down-hill through a course outlined by large rocks and boulders. In rainy times there are lots of moss, ferns, and pleasant water sounds. It looks quite dry now, faded moss and sad ferns. I see fluffy cream-colored blossoms mixed with poison oak vines climbing through bushes. I stop to take a picture, because it is a virgin's bower vine, lovely in the sunshine. It may be a contest among vines, as there are honeysuckle tendrils in there, too.

The trail crosses a section that has soft white rock and ash-like soil, then it enters a tree-shaded area. When it returns to sun, the soil is richer, the size, number and varieties increase, and I find myself in a bounteous place for flowers. There are legions of blossoms of all shades; purple, lavender and pink accompanied by white with blue, orange, cream, and a dazzling array of yellow sun cups.

Along the edges are myriad tiny flowers including the California plantain. It is delicately pretty, though inconspicuous in comparison to its dominant cousin, the English plantain, which has become so well naturalized it is a familiar park and garden pest. The native seems pale and wan next to the imported version. I look at the taller English import and think of the English gentlemen who came to Virginia in the early 1600s. The plantains' pointed buds remind me of their hats. Like some of those hats, the plant's pointy topper is adorned by a flourish of the finest, most delicate lace and feathers.

There is a wealth of blooms here of many kinds and colors...white and pink linanthus, blue and white sky lupine, yellow cream cups, gold fields and buttercups. Standing a bit taller is white yarrow. As always, white popcorn and yellow fiddleneck flowers are close. All of this is only a small part of the amazing beauties of Annadel Park. I stop at a bench where

I can admire the sight of coastal hills, still in their morning dress of blue with white mist and fading clouds.

Continuing the climb, I see the beginning of yellow blooms on monkey flower bushes. Nearby cheerful blue-eyed grass is having a fine time in the sun. A few Douglas iris lend support, and I am surprised to see two shade-loving woodland stars growing on the edge of a meadow. The flowers are dwarf in size, but there they are, toughing it out in the sun.

After a difficult, uneven, rock-filled stretch, I am out and up to the area I call the Viewing Place, with a wide full sight all around. I am high on a hill. There are other and higher places, but now is the time to stop and see this part of the world. Look to the west to see Santa Rosa and plains to more hills, look to the east and see those low mountains marching on to the north. Behind me and to the other side, meadows, hills and trees will coax you into seeing more of Annadel, a fine and wondrous place.

I commence the trip down, enjoying flowers, plants and trees as much as before. Everything looks new, fresh, and lovely. Tiring a bit, I think of Tom's Trek Stop bench below. I can see it is already in use by four young people, sitting on, and standing by it. One girl has a large white pit bull, leashed, but intimidating in aspect and size. It is against the law to bring dogs on park trails. I cross to the other side of the trail and look away as I pass. They become silent and watch as I go by, as does their companion, I think of as big Fido.

I have to take pictures of the colors as I hike down. The sky lupines are lovely, but it is the red-stemmed, pink-flowered fillarees that amaze. They fill the banks, meadows and trailsides with their bright blossoms. Lately, I have been captioning all the pictures in my files and I wonder about these. Fields of Fillarees, Fillaree Fields, Fillaree Filled Fields? So many choices.

After the Rain

At the beginning of November, after the first rains, I park in Annadel's parking lot at the end of Channel Drive and am struck by the patterns on the pavement. The first rains have washed fallen fir needles into designs, making a mosaic of the dark paving with waves of rusty needles. All of autumn is in this forest, and I am almost overcome with the beauty.

As I walk along Channel Drive, there are drifts of leaves on each side. The earlier leaves, deeper in the mounds and dampened by rain, have darkened to shades of brown. Those on the bottom, now almost black, are starting to blend into the earth. The later ones are colors of rusts and beige. Floating to the ground are the yellow leaves of the Oregon ash trees. Topping them all are the beautiful colors of the big leaf maple. Some of the leaves are eight to ten inches across and enhanced with splashes and shadings of rust and green against their autumnal yellow.

I am anxious to check one of my favorite plants, the gold back fern. It has that name because the back of each fern is heavily coated with yellow pollen. When the forest dries, this tiny fern goes into a sort of hibernation. It does not dry and wither like other ferns. The fronds fold into themselves like fingers into fists. The wiry, black stems will stand, topped by gold backed fronds, tightly furled. At the first rain, they unfold to salute the water, seeming as if they had never left. When my younger brother and I were children on many happy rambles in redwood forests, we encountered these ferns. We discovered, if the backs of the leaves were pressed to the backs of our hands, we would get a perfect imprint of the delicate fern. We never tired of seeing this depiction of the forest on our hands, and we happily renewed it every time we came.

While walking on Channel Drive, I come to a high bank, a favorite display place of plants, ferns and flowers. When damp, the moss of this bank is green and adorned at various times with scarlet Indian warriors, Mission bells, white rein orchids, yellow fairy lanterns and other treats. Always, in winter and early spring, the bank is lush with ferns. Today, to my delight, the gold backs are here again, greeting the damp, unfurling to display black stems and green leaves backed by gold. I restrain the temptation to stamp the back of my hand.

Nearby on the road, among downed leaves, a California newt, orange-bellied with brown back, is out on the pavement. I gently move him to the side of the road. As these newts do, when touched or threatened, this one plays dead, arching his back, displaying his orange side. He becomes still and stiff. I have seen too many flattened newts on this road to let him stay out on the paving. Of course, I know when I go he will do what he wants.

Tiny shoots of green grass and the first leaves of plants are sprouting along the road. In sunny spots, the green places are wider and the grass and plants higher. I stare at these green flourishes closely, looking for signs of the early blooming white-flowered milk maids, but it is too early and the leaves are too small.

The last time I walked here, the creek was low, in some places scarcely moving and covered with spent leaves. Now it is a creek that can be heard again. It is washing, running, and rippling over the rocks. It seems happy to be renewed and races forward, only pausing now and then to enrich the occasional deeper, darker pools.

I reach the ranger station and stop for a bit at the friendly table placed here for pauses like this. The sun is warmer, the sky is now blue and streaked by spare white clouds. Two turkey vultures take advantage of the warming air. They are in flight, dipping and soaring in the autumn sun. I watch for a while, having a good time with them.

The leaves in this sunnier area are drying. Oak leaves, browning and twisting as they dry, still show varying shapes and sizes. I see a large, deeply lobed black oak leaf with all its bristles intact. I lift it, feel the sharpness of the points, and twirl it in my fingers before releasing it to the autumnal drifts. The black oak acorns are the plumpest, round and fat with heavy cups. Blue oaks have thinner acorns, a bit more pointed. The coast live oaks have the smallest acorns, quite thin. Here and there, a round green seed of the California bay laurel tops the leaves. Soon the bay seeds will darken, looking like black olives when they fall.

In the shade, where the damp makes downed leaves darker, I see a fallen fir twig, the green gracing the leaves beneath it. A piece of an oak's dead branch, too, has fallen. It is completely covered with gray-white lichen, a striking contrast to the dark leaves.

The moss-encrusted boulders of two dry stream beds are now greener and waiting for more water to rush down to cover and enliven them. A snowberry bush, loaded with white berries, droops in front of the shaded rocks. The berries shine against the dark green moss. A small hill behind it is covered with downed leaves of every size and color. It is hard to absorb all of this autumnal feast.

Returning to the parking area, I go to a nearby table for lunch and brush away the covering of tiny fir pollen cones. In shape, they resemble the much larger seed cones, but these are less than an inch in length and are soft, carrying the pollen to fertilize the trees. Before the rains, they can sometimes be seen, downed, with a slight puff of pollen around them.

I rest, eat and watch my fellow hikers come and go. It is a Sunday, but people are scarce, and it is quiet here in the sun. I, too, am quiet, happy to be in the park and feel fortunate to be in this place, at this time, seeing and feeling it all.

Here and There

Going up Richardson Trail on an October day, I see poison oak as an exclamation point shining brightly red against green trees. Half hidden behind a stand of coyote bushes is a tall wild rose. I notice, because it is waving this year's crop of red hips in the morning breeze. Across the trail, honeysuckle vines with berries are doing the same as they cling to the tops of other bushes.

Autumn has arrived in Annadel Park. The blue oak leaves are joining with the black oaks, fluttering down on the trail. Together they add dashes of yellow, green and orange to the clutter of beige, brown, and rust needles and leaves already there.

Tiny primary leaves of spring plants, and green grass shoots, are sprouting trailside. I am fascinated by the sizes, shapes and diversity. Some are large enough to seem familiar. Surely these arrow-shaped ones must be next season's dock plants. Over here are some leaves resembling hedge nettles. Surprise, there is one lonely Philadelphia fleabane plant still holding a faded summer blossom. Not far away are some others keeping a few spent flowers. I see small clover and tiny lotus plants and there are yellow flowers on many false dandelions.

The canyon below the trail grows deeper and darker, and trees change from oaks to firs. When I reach a higher place on the hill, the ground flattens as it stretches to more hills, the oaks and grass return, and everything looks good in morning sunshine. Far off, some wild grapevines have turned a deep, autumnal red-purple. I found some the other day with raisin like grape clusters; also a few that were not yet dried. I tried them and, though sweet, they were so seedy I thought it

99

would take a lot of them to approach a meal.

Going left and entering Two Quarry Trail, I do not plan to go far, just to revisit some of it. Cyclists pass me, going up and coming down, as this is a popular way to go to Marsh Trail and Kenwood. I see only one other person on foot, a runner dashing uphill.

There are great slabs of basalt by the trail; giant, irregular slices. I am used to seeing myriad sizes and shapes, but these are something else. Puzzled, I stare for a while, my usual re-action. This park is a fine place for rocks and often sends me home to read more geology books, but I still know very little.

Nearby is a small level area where I saw lots of flowers last spring, including some hemlock plants. Now there are two of them left standing, tall, whitened and dry. I examine the dry stems, curious to learn if they retain the characteristic purple blotches on the stems. One has nothing, and the other have two or three dark spots. Not enough to mean anything. I must look for more dry hemlock plants.

After returning to Richardson Trail, I rest on a bench and study the remains of a nearby large, old, broken fir tree. It is quite remarkable in both size and lasting power. The downed branches are decaying, but still the stump stands tall and forbidding. I admire its strength and try to take pictures, though doubt I can capture the power of this remnant of an older forest.

As I walk down, I spot a tiny mushroom, reminding me of the little ones I called fairy mushrooms as a child. I find a fully formed white puff ball and another, just breaking through the ground. If fungus has arrived, fall is really here.

At the trailhead, I take a short side trip on Channel Trail to see a beehive I noticed a few weeks ago. It is a perfectly complete, large, oval beehive. I have no desire to see it up close, because it is accompanied by numerous bees. The bees seem large, active and, even at a distance, noisy.

Stopping at a park table and bench to have some water and a short rest, I am joined by a woman who remarks that she no longer walks far as she has arthritis. Suffering the same ailment, I commiserate. We chat a bit, and she goes on to relate that she has it because she ate too many cold things. I ask, "What cold things?" She replies, "Ice cream." I say, "That is interesting." Soon I say goodbye, as I feel a sudden urge to return home and eat large amounts of that deliciously autumnal pumpkin ice cream waiting in my freezer.

Out to Lunch

On April 3, I go in the Parktrail entrance, then walk down-hill to Spring Creek crossing. We have not had much rain, so it is good to hear the creek refreshed and alive again. Going toward Annadel Park I see tiny white linanthus flowers, pink fillaree and a few blooming yellow and purple sanicles along the trail.

It is a foggy morning and I think of hand warmers and a hot cup of coffee. Buttercups are everywhere and I try to think of them as warming sunshine.

I start up Spring Creek Trail for only a short way, in order to visit the lovely mission bell flowers blooming just around the corner. I greet them with a cordial, "You look great, beautiful as always," and think I detect a reciprocal glow.

Then I cross the bridge and head up Canyon Trail to see how the blue-eyed Mary blossoms are doing today. They have spread, covering more of the bank and hill, and are looking splendid. They are joined in their frolic by flowers of yellow, pink, blue and white. It seems to be a spring garden party gone wild.

The woodland strawberries are starting to bloom. I see many white blossoms, but have never seen a ripe, red strawberry in this park. I always look, hoping for just one delicious taste, but decided long ago that the birds are faster and have better eyesight. I am still looking. They are still winning.

The trail is rocky in the extreme. It is up and down and going from side to side all the way. My mood is lightened by spotting sun cups along the edges of the rocks. Slowly, I pole my way along, taking heart from these low-growing, brilliant yellow blooms.

As I walk, I see views of the Bennett Valley hills and beyond to the blue coastal hills in the distance. Closer are green
meadows, bushes, and trees, with convenient trails wandering
down the hills and across the meadows to this park.

I am headed to my favorite lunch place on this trail,
Tom's Trek Stop, a park bench with that name carved in the
back. I sit and enjoy my usual repast, half of a Cheddar-cheese

sandwich, half of a Fuji apple, and some water. Finished with
the first two courses, I ponder desserts. I am presented with a
choice: a little blueberry thing or a strawberry thing. Again,
I have the usual, both. I extend my appreciation to the chef,
myself, before leaving for my rocky downhill journey.

On my descent, the sun is shining, and there are more
and more flowers. Woodland pea vines are starting to bloom,
with clusters of pink and white flowers. Some oaks have added leaves to their present covering of varied lichens. Long
fishnet lichen streamers float in the hillside breeze. It has been
a lovely morning, a fine lunchtime and now, a remarkably
handsome afternoon presents itself.

At the Canyon Bridge bench, I talk with two female park volunteers who are on horseback. We are worried about bad erosion on the trails and talk about the upper portion of Spring Creek Trail and other places. We discuss and deplore the erosion caused by off trail bikers and, to a lesser degree, hikers.

I walk up the canyon part of the Vietnam Veteran's Trail and find it muddier after a recent rain. There is more water in the creek below. The moss is greener and the ferns are thriving. All in all, good news. There are even more flowers on the hill than last week, including a surprising amount of pink flowering plectritis. In damp places along the trail, the miner's lettuce is growing tall and blooming with little white clusters of flowers atop the round leaves. The early gold miners knew what they were about when they added these to their diet. The leaves are tender, with a pleasant taste, making good additions to a salad. The hilltop is lovely with various kinds of greenery and flowers of all colors. On the lower hillside is a gathering of orange California poppies surrounded by crowds of white popcorn flowers. Within the green field is a restrained riot of contrasting colors. Grateful for this day, I reluctantly leave these beautiful parks.

September Stroll

As I start up the W. R. Richardson trail in early September, I meet a delegation of wild turkeys, a large male followed by five females. The females have a tendency to scuttle, casting nervous looks as they go, but the male resents my intrusion on his parade. Clucking his displeasure he sends his best look of disdain as he stalks across the path. Noting his colorful plumage and large size, I consider telling the flock I am recommending him as a Thanksgiving treat, then decide against such an unfriendly gesture.

Everything is dust covered; the plants, bushes, rocks, the dust itself is dusty. The many human feet, horse's hooves, shuffling, struggling and striding up and down this hill, have churned the dirt to dust. The bike proprietors, wrestling their bikes uphill and racing them down, made generous contributions to this dusky haze. I look at it and think of the splendid winter mud to come.

The large leaves of a nearby mules-ear plant have bleached, dried and stiffened. The leaves in front lean down, and those in back stand, presenting a circular fan of pale autumn color. Honeysuckle berries are shading red, autumnal fir cones starting to fall, snow-berry bushes discoloring, commencing their leaf drop with their lustrous white berries still holding on. Up the hill a dead madrone tree stands, the leaves, now black and withered, its beautiful trunk still shining red-brown as before. Farther up there is a large wild rose bush with many hips, and I think of rose hip jelly.

This area is littered with small broken pieces of black obsidian. Seeing a larger piece, about two inches wide and one inch thick, I pick it up, look at it and consider the possibilities. I am not tempted to make an arrow head, so drop it on the path. Here, too, are many small lava pieces. They are a large part of the rocks on the trail.

I sit on a bench which has a view of a meadow and across to some of the hills on the other side of the valley. Today they look a misty blue, still topped with the morning's clouds. The sky is lightening with more blue, and a large cloud moves away from my view of sunlight. The meadow and hills take on a summer look. There are still clouds on the tops of some far hills, and a few white fluffs float in the sky, but soon it will be another warm day.

As the sun brightens the landscape, I notice an autumnal looking tree is really a fir almost engulfed in brightly colored poison oak vines. The top and a few branches remain free, but the rest resembles a deciduous tree changing color. This fir is smaller than others, and the few visible branches do not look vigorous.

Commencing a steeper climb, my pauses give opportunity to look down the hill into the trees below. There are many plants there, mostly sword ferns, and the wood ferns are still green in spite of the dryness of the hillside. On the hill above the trail are piles of cut rock, now moss covered. There is a quarry with wooden stairs leading to it and huge boulders bearing cut marks. Farther up, in more sunshine, the mossy rock piles have a light covering of dried summer grass.

The trail levels, coming to a picnic table, where I sit, take out water, bread, cheese, half an apple, and have lunch. I admire a nearby tree with red leaved poison oak vines grown halfway to the top. The noon sun is shining through the leaves, making them translucent, a glowing red. Nearby, hidden but heard, a crow gives an opinion of my intrusion.

Two bikers join me to wait for a third, and lay out a feast of trail bars. A biker, gesturing down a side trail, asks me,

"What's back there?" I reply, "That is Steve's S trail and is for hikers only, no bikes, no horses."

I return downhill through the forest of firs, redwoods, oaks and bay trees with its generous undergrowth of ferns. In spite of the dust covering everything near the trail, it is restful and lovely. This is where I saw calypso orchids last spring. I hope to see them again next year.

I hear the shouts and laughter of children behind me. Two little boys are running down hill with their parents hurrying behind. The boys, as always on hikes, are having more fun than their parents. Admonished, they slow, pause and, shouting, dash forward again. The family comes to a table and sits down for a welcome lunch break.

Just ahead a fir tree shelters the largest patch of Yerba Buena I have seen here. It has spread until it approaches the trail. In spite of its earlier vigorous growth, it is turning brown in the summer heat and dryness. I smell a leaf, and find only a hint of the usual healthy scent of mint. It grows throughout redwood country and near the ocean. An island in San Francisco Bay is named for it. Used as a medicinal herb by Indians, and pioneers, the early Spaniards recognized it and named it the good herb. It is still used today by people who know and appreciate its soothing, healing qualities. Nearby, a tall wild rose bush is reaching for a low fir bough. This rose must have had a goodly number of summer blossoms, as it is covered with red hips. I think of rose-hip tea garnished with a sprig of Yerba Buena.

I am again at the start of Richardson trail. I sit, drink water and, as always, look at the outsized poison oak vines that climb some of the nearby oak trees. One has a trunk four inches thick and climbs two-thirds of the way up a tree. The center of the tree is a tangle of vines, with only the ends of two branches and the top reaching out for sunlight. This vine is a bit larger than many, but you see these massive vines throughout the park. People really dislike this pesky vine. I wonder how the trees feel.

Lake and Lion

A windy day in December, trees bend, leaves and bits and pieces of this and that bounce, float and flutter from pile to pile, edge to path and back, then settle to await the next gust. I top my sweater with another, reach for my straw hat and, as the wind puts my hair on end, think better of it and step out without my fine old hat. I am not sure I can walk without the helpful skills of this treasured topper. I am more afraid of losing it than I am of losing myself. Off I go into the wilds of Spring Lake's well-paved and heavily trod paths and venture along to the closest lakeside bench.

I sit down to ease my Velcro-wrapped sore foot and survey my surroundings. The wind is blowing the lake into small waves and wavelets, causing it to be covered in lively little ruffles and rufflettes. It looks quite busy and I see ducks floating, diving and swimming. A few snowy egrets sit quietly on the far side, patiently waiting for sightings of unwary prey so they can catch a late lunch. Now and then a visiting seagull soars above looking for snacks to snatch.

Very few hikers are out on this windy afternoon. Those that are here seem to be a bit chilled, tightly buttoned, faces slightly reddened and hurrying on their way with or without companion dogs.

Feeling colder, I shuffle to the next bench, sit down and put up my foot. I am thinking this is far from a brisk, invigorating, healthful walk. Off I go again to another pause, to stare at the lake, hills and trees. I look up at the hills of nearby Annadel Park and wish I were up there trudging along. My hiking may be only a slow trudge, but it is much more satisfying and purposeful than this little shuffle.

A few days later, feeling much enriched and strengthened by wearing two real shoes, I embark on a walk taking me into Annadel. It is another freaky, late December day, warm with full sunshine. I start on Spring Lake fire trail and walk toward the Park. Feeling the warmth, I consider singing my version of "I'm Dreaming of a White Christmas." Having sympathy for the many others on this path, I go quietly.

Everywhere I look it is faded and dry. The willows growing in the creek bed are mostly leafless, the stems, now yellow. I think I see touches of white signaling the pussy willow blooms soon to be here.

Resting in the shade of a live oak tree, I stand and look at the nearby hills. A young couple stops. He says, "Are you waiting for the others to catch up?" I answer, "No, I am waiting for my breath to catch up." He laughs. She blurts, "I think you are so cute." Surprised, I smile and laugh. I consider her words as I thought I was wearing my usual odd, old eccentric look--denim jeans, plaid flannel shirt, battered walking shoes, straw hat and trusty hiking poles. Cute? I will have to rethink my image.

I continue to the bridge where this trail turns and reaches the edge of Annadel Park and North Rough Go Trail. I sit on a large rock, consider my ailing foot and decide to go no farther. Much as I love my hikes in beautiful Annadel, this is far enough for a first day in shoes.

I start back, look across the dry Spring Creek gully and remember the day I saw a mountain lion on the other side. I was surprised to see it in the middle of the morning, taking its ease, sitting and yawning on the horse trail. I had a theory that, if I hit my metal poles together, it would startle and frighten any mountain lions I chanced to encounter. On that theory, I clanged the metal poles, the sleepy lion startled and began to turn around and go back. Then, changed its mind and started into the ditch, heading toward my side. Happily, it slanted back and disappeared into a stand of willows and brush in the dry creek bed. I could see that clump of brush extended near more growth and live oaks by the trail. I stopped and waited for two walkers close behind to catch up and hurried along after them. Not answering my efforts to speak, they strode on, engrossed in important conversation, unaware of that lurking, extra-large pussy cat. I trotted along behind, immediately followed by a group of five bikers.

As I left that day, I told a passing park ranger about the lion. Hearing many such reports, he was not impressed, "It will soon go back into the park," he said, "They don't like to be around people." I thought then and think now, that people are not fond of being around them either. Seeing a mountain lion here once was just right. I don't need to see one again.

The People We Meet

Strange things happen in the Sonoma sun. I have met a few strange, and not so strange, people on Annadel State Park Trails. Most people encountered are fine and friendly. Cheery hellos, good mornings, have nice days are exchanged, with smiles all around, as we each pursue our day's activities. We have our times and places, and greet one another as we make our rounds. Sometimes those seen are a bit off in their way or what they say. Whatever it is, I remember those.

I recall when I was new to hiking the trails and walking in the park. While enjoying Channel Trail, I was startled when a man came from the trees and bushes and stood and talked at me,

"Are you having a good time, I am having a good time, yes, I like to walk in here, I think they are expecting me at home, I really should go home, I think I will walk some more, maybe I should be home, this is better, I like it more, yes, I think I'll walk, but not on these trails. I have better ways to go." I was muttering, "Uh hunh, uh hunh, maybe, if you say so."

He trotted away through the undergrowth, making his own trail as he tramped toward higher hills. He made me feel nervous, though I wished him well in his off-trail jaunt, knowing he should not do that as it is against park rules, and hoped to never meet him again.

One day, hiking up Cobblestone Trail and around the Orchard Loop and returning, tired and annoyed, as I had seen Orchard Loop on the trail map and had pictured a pleasant stroll through an old orchard, planted by a long ago land owner. Visions of apple blossoms in my mind, I slogged through a steep, rocky, difficult loop. There were some fine native trees,

112

but in the main, it had rock-mining pits, piles of rocks, and rocks extending into the trail. Near the top, one pit had filled with water. I wondered how deep, is it just winter's rain or is there a spring? No one else had been dim enough to take this trail, so there was no one to ask.

I was slowly and carefully making my way down a rocked-over spot on Cobblestone, when I met a middle-aged man pushing his bicycle uphill. He did not seem to be having a good time. I said hello and commented that it got worse as you went higher. He grunted and gave me a look saying foolish old lady, what do you know? Ten minutes later he passed me going down, still pushing the bike. He did not look my way, and did not so much as grunt when he passed. I restrained my laughter, but had pleasant chuckles all the way down the hill. Still do.

Quite some time ago, on my first visit to North Burma Trail, I met a man coming down who told me he hiked this trail a lot, it was great, and somewhere farther up was a waterfall. I thanked him and renewed my efforts to get up the hill. This was before I had hiking poles, and I was even more careful and slow.

A biker going by me from below said, dourly, "What are you doing on the hardest trail in the park?" I replied, "I want to go up and see the waterfall." He said, contemptuously, "There is no waterfall!" I was crushed, sat down on one of the many rocks, thought about it and decided to give it up. Since then I have seen the waterfall and learned it is not the hardest trail. I still think of the scornful man on a bike and am still annoyed.

Recently, walking down Spring Creek Trail, I encountered a fellow watching three turkeys through binoculars. He said to me, "The male turkey directs the females by movements of his body and tail." He went on to explain that, if the male's tail moved one way, the females went to the right, if another way, they move to the left. I watched a bit until the turkeys exited into bushes. I have a way with turkeys, as they generally leave when they see me. The gentleman moved up the trail with bike and binoculars. He did not seem strange but had a most unusual pastime of interpreting turkey tail talk.

Last year, while walking on the Ridge Trail between Howarth and Spring Lake Parks, I met a man I had seen on other trails. He was leading his elderly, very friendly, large dog. He stopped to tell me about a strange-looking man with a large stick farther down this trail who had made threatening gestures as he and his dog walked by.

Thinking about it, I decided to continue as it may have been the stranger did not like dogs. I found him beside the trail, in the bushes, back turned, seeming to be answering a call of nature. I hurried on past, glad of his diversion, wondering how much poison oak there was in those bushes.

About a month ago, coming down W. R. Richardson Trail in the afternoon, I met an elderly woman using walking poles, slowly climbing up the hill. I said hello and continued down.

Around a curve was an even older gentleman using one long pole, struggling up hill. He took a small step, stopped for a bit then, took another step. He carried a small backpack. I said hello; he didn't answer. It seemed he needed all his strength and every breath to proceed slowly, oh so slowly, up that steep hill.

I looked a few times as I walked, and it was step, pause, step, pause as he forced himself on. Noticing how the elderly lady was watching to measure his progress, I thought how they may have enjoyed walks up here for many years, too, and now, even though age and infirmity had slowed them both, they still wanted to climb these hills to see and enjoy the places they had visited together in better times.

Summer Snapshots

In mid-June, I go up W. R. Richardson Trail. Yellow Klamath weeds and star thistles are growing almost everywhere now. The thistles are bright, and the Klamath weeds are pretty, though both are invasive pests. Ferns continue to droop and wither in the shaded parts of a now dry creek. It is easy to see summer is here. The cream bushes are in bloom, their flowers floating puffs of delicate cream against a backdrop of green. The woodland pea vines' tiny leaves and stems stand out against the dark forest floor.

Spring colors are mostly going or gone. The blue Ithuriel's spear is still blooming, fading but game, brightening drying meadows and forest. It is a remarkably pretty and tough little plant.

A downhill hiker tells me there is a mother turkey with six chicks around the next bend. I near the place, hear the turkey mother clucking, but she and the chicks hide in a thicket of coyote brush. As I near, they retreat deeper into the dense bushes. Today will not be my day for baby turkey viewing

The blossoms of tiny trailside flowers are gone, but the little plants are there, green and persistent, building seeds for next year. Tall dock plants, with wide leaves and green seeds, stand out against dry grass. Last fall, the dock had rusty brown seeds, and later, winter's plants held tattered leaves and espresso-colored-seeds.

Early in July, I hike on the west side, going in through the Parktrail entrance. It is usually sunny and breezy on top of this hill. I admire the lichen-laden trees and think it must be the moisture in the winds that makes lichen so abundant up here.

After walking for a time, I reach Spring Creek Trail.

Such a roaring deluge last winter, though now the water only trickles and puddles, a murmur not a roar.

At some time in the past, a land movement caused the creek to split, and water flows on both sides of a small piece of land. I think a part of the hill might have slid to form the boulder-covered island. This mini-isle is covered with trees. Among them is a small maple, almost a bonsai shape, not very tall, wide for its height, and a bit crooked. At this moment the little tree is handsome in dappled sun and shade.

Going up, I meet a man on horseback, and move over to make room for him to pass me on the trail. He asks, stopping his horse, "What do you think about this trail?" "Not bad here, but the top part is terrible, eroded, worn and rocky," I say. He agrees. We chat a bit about possible causes and solutions. He thinks he will go to meetings and agitate for change. On this hopeful note, we part.

There are two female deer standing on the hill. I am much more impressed with them than they are with me. Arriving at the now dry creek crossing, I find it is strewn with rocks and boulders. I look for one of the right size and sit for a while, considering the steep, difficult trail ahead. I know that going to the top is hard, but coming down is worse, and I decide not to do it today.

I walk down to cross the bridge leading to Canyon Trail, and start up the back way to the Vietnam Veteran's Park. Down by the creek, cream bushes are still blooming with unusually large flowers, admirable in the noontime sunshine. They get lots of water by the creek, and the plants themselves are large. The Pacific nine bushes are thriving here too.

Farther up the hill are several service berry bushes with red berries. A branch close to the trail has one almost purple berry. Lightening the berry crop, I taste it. One of my plant

117

books said the Indians ate them, though they are seedy and rather tasteless. I agree with that description. Another book states they are sweet and jelly can be made from them.

On the top there is a buckeye tree, still holding a few of the many white flowers that decorated it in spring. It is late for flowers, as some of these trees have already started to shed their leaves.

In early August, I take a short walk into Annadel Park along Channel Drive. If you haven't much time, this is a pleasant, quick trip with a flowing stream, redwoods, many oaks, other trees, bushes and plants, occasional wildlife and, always, an interesting cast of characters.

As I start, I see a narrow strip on the right side of the paving that holds numerous small plants of nightshade. I always check on their progress, and discover a few, slightly taller than the others, with tiny white flowers. One tall plant, left from last year, still thrives in this unlikely location, holding both flowers and shiny dark berries. I wish it well since growing here, it may be flattened by auto tires at any time. Each year, many are squashed, but they prove their resilience by returning.

Farther along, some Philadelphia fleabane plants grow in deepening shade. They are neither thriving nor blooming this year. I remember a few years ago, a cyclist kept running over them. Instead of staying on the trail above, he rode down this small bank. I became increasingly annoyed as he destroyed more plants and dug deeper ruts into the soft soil.

I never saw him, just the result of his shortcuts. When no one was around I would pick up sticks and branches and throw them over his deepening trail. They could be seen from his start at the top of the bank, but my efforts were useless as he rode over those, too. I kept trying and he kept returning. Winter storms came and an old, dead tree fell across that bank. Destiny! A few lesser trees and branches came with it, all across his path. Pleasing, as my best efforts could never have produced such splendid results.

A small maple, with yellowing leaves, at the bottom of a hill presents a pleasant contrast to the bays and oaks behind it. A wind starts to blow, and the shifting green reveals a larger yellowed maple growing higher on the hill. Nearby are tall plants of poison oak with red leaves, now flaming by thickets of gray, broken stems. A large snowberry bush is in front, the berries white against browning leaves. With the colors, a cooler morning, and the wind, I feel autumn growing closer.

Chill Factor

I drive to Spring Lake in December, using the main entrance because there are so many friendly benches close to that parking lot. I'm planning to sit on a bench and look at the lake, while waiting for my ailing foot to have better days. It is eleven o'clock in the morning and there is, as yet, no sunshine. The clouds are so dark, they seem almost purple in places. I look for a bench, sit down, and shiver in the cold wind. This is not a promising start to a pleasant afternoon by the lake.

Nearby is a small congregation of Canadian geese, gabbling softly to one another while they gulp blades of grass or weeds or bugs or whatever it is they are busily grabbing and swallowing. Whoever named a gathering of geese a gaggle must have met a Canadian goose. To listen to them is to hear a gaggle. When they are not loudly hooting, they are muttering google, giggle, gaggle, gaggle, gugg. In a silent answer to their mutters, I think, of course, fellows, I understand, if I am not here to feed you, I should leave. So I do.

I move to another spot, but it is no more hospitable, not at all like Spring Lake Park's usual welcoming smiles. Giving up, I drive uphill to leave this park, and the sun begins to shine as the clouds fade and drift away. Not enough. I still feel cold and consider where to go.

I decide to drive into Annadel Park to see how the ferns are looking today. As I drive by the roadside banks, usually fern covered by December, I slow my car and creep along so I can see the few ferns growing. The polypodies are scant and looking a bit sad. Not at all their usual attitude of, "We will cover all this ground and then wave at passersby."

There are as yet no maidenhair ferns, as they do not make their entrance until there is a good supply of moisture. The gold back ferns are still open, but seem tentative. The moss looks shrunken in size and yellowed in color. There is no water in any of the seasonal creeks usually coming down the hills at this time.

I drive to the parking lot, stop and get out, considering a slow limp along Channel Drive. Too cold, I return to the car, which now seems warm and cozy, and look at the surrounding trees. Almost all the deciduous trees have lost their leaves. Some blue oaks retain faded leaves in their higher branches. When a gust hits the tree, the dry, bleached and bent remnants flutter down, slowly at first, seeming to accelerate as they near the ground. When they land in the dusty lot, they scatter, blown one way and another, making rustling whispers as they skitter about.

Nearby, trees bereft of leaves display their twisted, curving, mossy branches. Oaks without their spring and summer covering are surprisingly contorted. Each winter I am amazed and fascinated by their unique shapes.

I move my car to the horse trailer parking side of this lot, as there are no horses or trailers in sight. From here, there is a better view of the tall trees growing on these hills. On the hill to my right, a flock of turkeys approaches a rail fence. The lead bird hops to the top to consider any activity that might not be to their liking. Seeing nothing, he jumps down and advances around my car. There is some barking from a leashed dog, and the turkey goes back over the fence to join his fellows, all of whom continue their browsing uphill away from the departing dog and the few parked cars.

The tops of the heavy fir trees are beginning to bend to the increased strength of this afternoon's wind. I start the engine and drive out along the creek where the alders, too, are bare. They retain their dangling green catkins for next year, reminding me of the pleasant warmth of spring time to come.

Silence and Sounds

I enjoy solitary walks and hikes in Annadel Park, the serenity under the trees while walking on the soft forest duff, no barking, no talking, shouts or laughing. Occasionally a wind soughs through the branches overhead, a tree moans as the wind increases and rubs one limb against another, a snatch of birdsong as you pass. All of those familiar sounds complete my pleasure and content. There are lovely silences in which

to reflect on life and the beauty and natural grandeur of this place. When thinking of the quiet times, I sometimes remember, too, the noise, usual and unusual, I have heard when here.

There are bird sounds, though not many, as most birds like to stay away from people, preferring to distance themselves from humans. An exception are the noisy crows. They enjoy sitting above visitor's heads, screaming, shouting, insulting those who pass below. If no people or animals are near, they shout at one another. Noise is their work, their pleasure, their reason for being. At times the flock will fly together, wheeling about in unison, graceful in flight, though still giving noisy squawks as they look for new targets.

Squirrels are less cautious than birds and will stay in the branches, chittering at one another. Squirrels, like crows, tend to scold. Much less cautious than birds, they will stay in the branches scolding humans, birds and each other. Sometimes they are quite excitable, raising their voices in condemnation of another's behavior, or shouting in outrage at humans cluttering the ground beneath their trees.

Occasionally you might hear snatches of birdsong, sweet sounds of joy. More often, there will be the knocking sounds of woodpeckers as they pound their beaks against reluctant old oaks. They drill holes, push in acorns, and later come back to retrieve them.

When you go to nearby lakes, you see resident ducks and geese are little intimidated by humans. Rather than flying away in fright, they gather round in hunger, begging for handouts. The geese hoot loudly to attract attention. In the woods and on the trails funny, self-important turkeys gobble a bit in quiet mutters or loud warnings, then hurry under bushes to hide. Turkeys are humorous in their comments, conversation, and general behavior. Watching them strut or scuttle can make you smile. I think of them as obnoxious, but funny.

Most walkers, hikers and runners give greetings depending on their speed and the steepness of their climb. Everything from hi, gasp, hello, wheeze, mumble to full-throated good morning and goodbye. The sport of running requires concentration and good breathing techniques, as demonstrated to me one day near the bottom of Canyon Trail. A group of high-school girl runners were dashing downhill clad in running gear and evenly matched in size and appearance. Running and talking as they passed at good speed, none missed a step or a syllable as they went by.

Some bikers, coming from behind, will shout, "On your right. On your left." Others like to zoom by, thus providing excitement for your day. Sometimes we have short conversations. I recall a brief talk with a cyclist I met at a lower part of Canyon Trail. He had stopped and was leaning forward over his bike. Concerned, I said, "Are you all right?" "Yes, just out of shape," he replied, "But I need to exercise." I cautioned, "Don't try to do too much, too soon." We talked about the damage done to the trail by the winter's heavy rain. I, the pessimist, said, "This is a rocky mess." An optimist, he surveyed the trail and replied, "It's a rock garden."

In some ways too many people behave exactly as they do on the outside streets, talking and texting on their phones, seemingly unaware of the beauty surrounding them. How sad, to miss so much of what the world has to offer.

Sometimes the hum of traffic from outside can be heard. Many times I have heard sirens from distant streets, reminders we are not far away from our lives; no matter how far or fast we go, we'll soon return to real time and place.

Some trails, being more difficult, are less heavily traveled, giving many opportunities for quiet listening. The joy of nature is speaking to you, especially in the silence. Be grateful for a quiet time, because noise will soon return.

Some sounds are intrusive and others have charm. Some of the best are the voices of children having fine times walking and running on the trails.

There are horses in the park; most are calm and used to meeting people. An occasional horse will be nervous, jittering and snorting when encountering someone on a trail. I stand well back and wait for the rider to guide it ahead. Horses are seldom heard, but do leave numerous gift mounds on the trails for people to avoid.

I meet friendly people, and sometimes talk for a bit. It may only be a few words or a discussion of our walks and what we have seen. Sometimes I just go along, quietly enjoying the words and ways of those I meet. Most people I like, a few, not so much. All in all, though meetings are brief, they are quite pleasant.

Cyclists slowly and laboriously work their way to the top, because they know how good it is to race down. One memorable day, when nearing the entrance to Richardson Trail, I heard yells and shouts coming down the hill. They sounded happy; these were not sounds of fright or consternation. I had never heard calls like these as bicyclists generally enjoy their rides in silence.

Here they came and what fun they were having, a group of young men, riding fast, vocal in their enjoyment of speed. None wore helmets, the usual biker's outfits, or used caution. They skidded down and sped around the gate and onto Channel Drive, still whooping and hollering as they raced toward Santa Rosa. Not at all in the style of most cyclists who display quiet enjoyment of downhill speed. Though they were rude and rowdy, I still remember the noise and enthusiasm of their descent.

Season's End

It is the end of spring and the start of summer. A walk through Annadel Park's dried and drying grass and flowers will convince anyone of that. My favorite season, how I hate to see it go.

In June, I stroll along Channel Trail, an easy, pleasant place to see spring flowers. There has been recent work done on this trail, spreading gravel in last winter's wet and muddy places. Now the trail is not flowing like a small creek, but is dry and dusty. I see the lovage plants are still green but with yellowing edges, the seeds ready to fall. Almost all the grass is dry except the foxtail, which is barely green and holding its seeds to stick on passing animals and people.

On the hillside, there is an occasional yellow mariposa lily, some blossoming white yarrow, many strangely named, bright blue Ithuriel's spear flowers, and lots of pretty pink clarkias. I miss the wine cup and elegant clarkias that bloomed here last year at this time. However, I see some large plants of lavender coyote mint. I would like to rub a leaf and smell the strong fragrance of mint, but can't reach any as they are growing within a clump of poison oak.

I walk the length of the trail, and in the few still damp and shady places, I see the ferns are gone or going. There is some maidenhair at the bottom of banks where a little water continues to drain. There are tiny white flowers on one of my favorite plants, Yerba Buena, so I rub a leaf and enjoy the mint aroma.

Later, for a Sunday hike, I go up Spring Creek Trail, knowing it starts as a pleasant stroll through the woods, but gets quite steep and rocky in the second half. In April and early May there were several mission bells blooming near the start of the trail. The flowers are gone and in their place are interesting and unusual seed pods. Climbing, I miss seeing flowers that were here a short time ago.

There is still a little water in this part of Spring Creek and, nearing the small dam, I hear water spilling over the top. A young man in a white T-shirt is seated near the dam in what, from my viewpoint, seems to be the lotus position, head bowed, concentrating on printed material in his lap. I pass quietly.

Here are some large, partially withered leaves by the trail. I stop and verify they are the remains of two recently blooming trilliums and am sorry I missed seeing two of my favorite flowers. I saw them often as a child living in the Humboldt County redwoods during the early 1930s.

Soon, I am into the rocky climb, and am careful to have secure footing as I climb higher and must stop every few feet to look at the surroundings. If anyone is coming on the trail, I gladly stand aside for them, as it gives me more time to look at everything. Even the rocks are fascinating, so much lava and conglomerate and sandstone. What could that large, glittering rock be. I wish I knew more about rocks. Sometimes I read geology books only to realize how little I know and will never know. Rocks are hard to understand, plants are easier. I wish I knew a geologist who wanted to know flowers. We could trade details.

A few flowers are scattered here and there along the trail. Spring Creek Canyon is dry, and this rock-strewn hillside is even drier. Still, I see flowers of yellow, blue and white, now enhanced with yellow-orange monkey flower bushes and small, yellow, daisy-like flowers called butterweed.

There are blooming bushes with lovely white sprays at the end of fine-leaved branches. I think they are chemise and, just before the lake, I see two pearly everlasting plants with white blooms.

In the lake are one small child wading and eight Canadian Geese swimming. I walk across the dam to find a place to sit in the shade. A female hiker busy texting, nods when I ask to sit at the other end of a large table with benches. I enjoy some water and a short respite from all that onward and upward action. I feel the heat increasing, so don't stay long, but move on toward Canyon Creek Trail.

In the beginning, many trees are supplying shade, and the trail isn't as rocky and difficult as it is farther down. A spring along the way with a sizable, barrel-like trough, supplies water for horses. Water from the spring above also trickles down to a large and beautiful woodwardia fern luxuriating in the damp. A culvert under the trail carries excess water down to more woodwardias. On top of a hill, where Marsh Trail starts, is a table with benches under a blue oak tree. I eat my lunch, chatting with bikers stopping for a short break.

I return to a section of this trail I think of as The Viewing

Place, and what a view it is. It seems one can see all of Santa Rosa, out to the western hills, and more hills and mountains to the east and north, the distance making the farthest seem a distant, darker shade of the blue sky. I leave the tranquility of this special place and approach a badly eroded section that returns me to watching every step I take.

Faster, younger, stronger hikers trot, hike, walk and run past me. I shift from side to side of the road, looking for level places, judging the amount and size of rocks and gullies against the sliding of small rocks and gravel. I have been up and down here many times, but forget how difficult it is for me. It grows increasingly warm, and I look forward to the lower, more shaded portions, steeper and rockier though they may be. I am cheered by the blue flowers of Ithuriel's spear, and the grassy hillsides are starred with the gorgeous, golden Mariposa lilies. There are not many flowers left, but the colors are amazing. In a trailside ditch there are what may be the last of this season's delicate, pale-blue flax flowers.

Finally, I reach the bottom, cross the bridge, and pass where I began at Spring Creek Trail. More walking and climbing to get out of the park is needed, so I leave, taking time to pause along the lower creek and admire the cream bushes with their fine racemes of creamy white flowers. They remind the very tired me why I love and enjoy these difficult hikes. It is always the joy and beauty of what I see and experience in nature that keeps me planning my next hike.

Uphill and Down

On the third of March, I take a short, pleasant stroll, searching for wildflowers. Beginning at Annadel Park's ranger station, I enter Channel Trail, which always has lots of spring flowers, and reach a small hillside meadow where, in season, many varieties grow and bloom. I am a bit too early and see only a few milk maids and two shooting stars.

It is distressing to see a vandal biker has taken looping off-trail rides up and down this small hill, and the grass is uprooted, rocks shoved aside and soil cut open. The next rain will turn these ruts into eroding streams of water and mud, making the cuts wider, deeper and longer. I am angered by what has been done and sickened when I see the depth of the cuts through the place where royal larkspur grew in previous years. It is difficult to concentrate as I keep thinking of the desecration of this spring flower garden. I see this often, but today makes me feel quite discouraged.

I remember an oso berry patch by the creek, and go over to see if there are blossoms. Seeing there are, I pause quietly, inhaling the fragrance of the drooping clusters of white bell-like flowers, until I feel calmed and refreshed. Returning to my parking place, I notice the black oaks show signs of leafing, and decide to climb to the top of Richardson Trail where many of these trees grow.

Going uphill is slow for me, and younger, stronger, faster hikers hurry past. It is a steep struggle for some cyclists, still they are faster too. It is a pretty climb, lots of fir and oak trees, nice views of moss and ferns in a creek bed, and, in sunnier spots, the pretty milk maids are growing and blooming.

At the entrance to Two Quarry Trail, there is a bench, and I sit for a time. When presented with an opportunity, I always rest a bit, as it is helpful in these climbs to pause occasionally. After my last hike up Spring Creek Trail, I wondered if I had come to a time when I should curtail some of my lengthier wandering. I think of all the reasons why, make no decision and start walking again.

The next section, one of my favorites, passes through a grove of redwoods. I observe the beauty and enjoy my time here, giving myself over to the spirit of this place. On the way, there is a small sunny clearing with table and benches. Nearby is a partially downed black oak which still lives. The new leaves are opening and show the lovely, soft, velvety rose color I have been anticipating. Having fresh energy, I renew my hike driven by the old motto: onward and upward.

I stop at the next table for water and a brief rest. A young woman there stops her stretching exercises when I come and asks, "Are you walking alone?" I answer, "I do not know anyone who wants to do this. I am slow, stopping to look at everything, and most hiking groups want to go fast. It is better I go at my own speed."

When I reach the seat at the top, I find a gentleman there enjoying the fine view and his lunch. He gives permission to share the view and bench. We talk, and I tell him about the oaks before I leave to look at them, and find I am a week or two early for these trees. I do see pretty blue hound's tongue flowers, yellow buttercups ,and white milk maids in the green grass by the trail. It has been a long, steep climb, but I feel invigorated with fresh spring energy.

When returning through the redwoods, I see a familiar face coming up. The cyclist I recognize from walks on the west side, stops and says, "Didn't I just see you on the other side? You are all over the place." I laughingly reply, "I try." He says, "It's great. Keep it up." He pedals up and I walk down.

Near the end of the redwood section, I spot another familiar person, a park ranger in his truck. He stops and says it is nice to see me again, up here and enjoying myself. We talk about the black oaks and spring wildflowers. I tell him it is beautiful and I love it here and, again, off we go, each on our own path.

I hike on down reflecting on this lovely day, the great things I have seen, the fine, friendly people I'm getting to know, and the new ones I have yet to meet. I have been in the park five hours, and have walked about five miles. My decision on whether to keep hiking these trails has been made. The cyclist's last words to me, "Keep it up," seem to be the answer.

Rainy Day Memories

During rain, I often sit by a front window watching the water bouncing into a nearby pond, splattering on walkways and dripping down trees. While enjoying this natural wonder, I think of others I have seen and felt while walking in the nearby hills of Annadel Park. There are favorite places I hope to soon see again, and the faintly weird, strange, unusual and memorable times, places, and days I'd like to repeat, and those I would not.

I remember one day's hike up W.R. Richardson Trail. The day was cloudy and cool, no rain in the forecast, so I was warmly clad in jacket and straw hat. As I neared the top of the first section, an area with a large meadow, the rain commenced. I started by moving from tree to tree, walking faster to take refuge under the limbs, then moving on to the next tree. When walking uphill, the limit to how fast I can walk is low. There I was, moving in a slow hustle from shelter to open and back to shelter. Making it to a higher part of the trail where, surrounded and safely under dense redwoods, I could pause, breathe and proceed at my usual slow uphill pace. It is no wonder redwoods are among my favorite trees.

With pleasure, I think of the easy Channel Trail that runs parallel above Channel Drive. A site not far from the ranger station is home to many spring-blooming wild flowers, an amazing number and variety of flowers in this small area. It was here, I first saw the little flowers variously named seldom-seen blue-eyed Mary and few-flower blue-eyed Mary, and spinster Mary. Since then, I have seen many in various places and found that, though numerous, their bloom is brief. Perhaps they should be called look-fast-at blue-eyed Mary.

My favorite wildflower memory and favorite place are

the same, on North Burma Trail. There is a fern-covered hill above, and a small waterfall below where the water drains down a rocky flower-covered bank and then on to the lower creek. So many flowers, all lovely. There are white blossoms on cream bushes, and the hydrangea-like Pacific nine bush. I like to recall the beauty of tiny, yellow fairy lanterns, and a nearby contrast in the deep, bright color of royal blue lark-spur. The background sounds are of a creek rushing down its rock-strewn course. A magic place I hope never to forget. When I can no longer come to see these hills I will remember.

One spring, I decided not to take the Orchard Loop, but to take the longer Cobblestone Trail. I did not see anyone, and felt slightly anxious as I walked. It is somewhat difficult with lots of rocky places, but fine trees and shady vistas. I saw the remains of a well-built campfire in the middle of the trail. I say well-built, because the logs and sticks had been carefully placed, and the wood used had been cut with a hatchet from a small dead fir tree.

All through the hike, I felt ill at ease. I thought it had been because I was alone out there. However, there was some-thing more I learned two weeks later; if I had known I would not have gone that way. In conversation, a ranger mentioned there was a pair of mountain lions with two cubs living in that area. I don't think a lot about the park's wild-life, though I do believe in being sensible and cautious. Sometimes I wonder if when I felt as if I might be watched, I had been.

I remember once starting on Louis Trail and turning back because it seemed deserted and it was almost five in the afternoon. I took well-traveled Richardson instead. Louis' wandering will take you from the lake to North Burma Trail, which leads you to the top of Richardson Trail, and so down the hill and out. In springtime, Louis Trail has lots of wildflowers.

Thinking of Spring Lake Park, I remember the crowd of crows living and thriving there. I have never before heard so many, so loud or often as these Lakeside residents. I cannot think of the place without remembering those noisy crows.

The best things by that lake may well be all the charming children. Every time I walk there, I see pretty little people. During my last walk, I saw a beautiful child whose mother was trying to coax her into her stroller in order to return home. The child kept refusing while leaning against a pole. Slowly, she began sliding up and down, rubbing her back on it. When I laughed the mother said, "Just like a little bear." Later, I saw them walking away, the child, still not in the stroller, now happily holding the leash of their small dog, confusing it while trying to lead it as they left.

When I think of small children and walks in the park, I always return to those I saw playing in lower Spring Creek. I was walking on the Parktrail entrance to Annadel when I saw them in their watery adventure. Three or four weeks earlier the creek had been rushing down here, so high, it could not be forded. It had less force, but I thought it rather high for a child. A girl who looked to be about six years old and a boy, about eight, were in the water. Both barefoot, they wore blue pajama bottoms, she with a dress on top, he with a T-shirt. Neither had a sweater or jacket and, though the sun shone, the air felt cool.

He was in the middle of the creek watching her. She stood on a small log, brought down by earlier high water, now caught between two boulders and held by them across the creek. She was jumping up and down calling to her brother, "Nyah, Nyah, look at me, look at me!" He turned away, the log, freed by her jumping, twisted and started downstream. She fell back into the water. I started to her, but immediately she jumped to her feet, yelling at him, "Nyah, Nyah, not hurt, not hurt."

Soaked, she waded downstream to a neighborhood swing suspended from an oak tree, now hanging over the widened creek. She climbed from the water into the swing and commenced swinging back and forth, higher and higher. The boy waded to shore, walked to a tall clump of grass and weeds and, back turned, appeared to be relieving himself. They seemed to be all right, even though I thought they were the wrong age, at the wrong place at the wrong time. It was about ten in the morning on a school day.

Why were these children in this place? Why weren't they in school? I remembered the childhood wildness of my brother and myself. Troubled, I thought, at least we would have been in school at this time of day. After school, on weekends, would we have done this? Probably, but not while dressed in pajamas.

Adrift in Time

Feeling a bit down and dour, I start a September walk at the shaded east end of Channel Trail. It's so dusty even a slow step will bring up an ankle-high cloud. Pieces of obsidian on the path bring memories of childhood walks in Lake County where rocks from the volcano of Mt. Konocti are scattered as they are here. Bikes go by and I notice the pieces of obsidian are becoming increasingly shattered. In places the wear has reduced it to a peppering of shiny black spots.

A pleasant cyclist passes, I stand aside and he says, "Thank you, dear." I reply, "You're welcome," and restrain the impulse to add a "sweetie" to that.

Here are a few hazelnut bushes and, as always, I stop to admire the soft, fuzzy leaves and look for a nut. I never see them and assume the squirrels are always there first. To my surprise I find one and pocket it. As I do, I remember when I was a child in Humboldt County and my brother and sister and I would look for them.

If Scott or I could find one we would quickly break it between two rocks and eat it then and there. If our older sister found them she would squirrel them away in her pockets, take them home, crack them with a neat and tidy nut cracker and enjoy the luxury of a small stash.

I used to marvel at all that control and recall how she picked and ate fresh crab. In the depression years Humboldt Bay Dungeness crab was sold at the Eureka docks for ten cents apiece or three for twenty-five cents. Knowing the crab munching proclivities of his offspring, my father generally purchased three and we would have a crab dinner. Scott and I, impatient as always, would pick a little and eat a little, but Edwyna would carefully pick and stockpile and pick and wait and pick some more. When her crab pile became high enough she would add chopped lettuce and some salad dressing and have a feast. I look back at our childhood and all of our competition, contests, fun and games, giggles and good times and am comforted on this dry, early autumn day.

I pass a tall bank, in winter and spring adorned from top to bottom with ferns and graceful cream bushes. Now it is giving a new aspect to the words "withered" and "sere." It looks parched, dusty and sad. The gold back ferns are gathered into tight, dry fists and appear as if it will take more than a brief shower to make them release their grip.

In sunnier spots bracken is already brown; here in shade it is only wilting and faded. The sword and wood ferns seem limp, with less life than the last time I came here.

I can't find a single leaf of the fragrant Yerba Buena plants that flourished near the path last spring. They will be back, but I miss seeing and smelling them.

I look up to be reassured by the green canopy. On the hill, sunshine lights the dark leaves of a coast live oak. The blue sky brightens as the morning clouds recede. The sunshine has not yet touched down here, but there is increasing warmth.

An old and giant fir stands a distance above the trail. Its large roots are above ground where the path crosses the hill. One root has been polished so much by hiker's feet and cyclist's tires it is now as shiny as an old table. It is a handsome piece of wood, but a few inches higher the root has begun dripping sap and I wonder if this may be in protest of the constant, intrusive wear.

I pass the no longer used Oakmont waste-water pond, now greatly diminished and reduced to a large shallow puddle edged with a red algae-like substance and dry, caked black and gray scum. Today there are no ducks floating on the water. I have seen occasional ducks here and worry about their health.

It's All Good

Presented with another lovely spring day in March, I drive into Annadel Park to the large parking lot where there is a horse event in progress. Several horse trailers are parked and more are arriving. A travel trailer and an adjoining taped off area have what seem to be preparations for a picnic and/or barbecue. Looks interesting, but since I haven't received my invitation, I begin a walk uphill on Richardson Drive to Lake Ilsanjo.

I try to hurry through the shade and linger in sunshine as the morning air is cool, and to enjoy the familiar sights along the trail. Two small Oregon grape bushes have clusters of remarkable, bright-yellow blossoms, handsome against the shiny, dark leaves. Every sight, every vista may be one I have seen many times, but each time it seems new and lovely. Stopping often, seeing a bloom or a shaded view of lichen and moss in soft colors, everything seems fresh, new, and lovelier than the last time I visited.

I sit for a minute on a bench with a pleasant view of hills, close and distant. Turkeys in nearby coyote bushes sound off to one another. Soon I am having another brief respite on a bench near the entry to Two Quarry Trail and wondering about that trail. Last year a hiker told me he had seen a patch of calypso orchids growing there. I want to look, but the entrance always seems dark and lonely.

As I continue, there is a flash of yellow on one side. It is a tall Johnny Jump-Up plant with a lone blossom. It has interesting divided leaves, and I soon see one more on the other side of the trail. There are some wild raspberry bushes across the way, and I resolve to check them in summer for berries. Here are some beautiful white camas lilies. Two women stop

141

to look and ask about the lilies that are growing by several blue Douglas Iris. One woman asks if the deer will eat the lilies. I assure her they will not as they are poisonous. Deer know poisonous plants and never try so much as a nibble.

Pollen is included in the spring festival of blossoms, and I add a few sneezes to the sounds of spring. On the way down the steep path to the lake, I admire the shaded ferns in a small fir forest above the trail. Below is a dry creek bed cluttered with mossy boulders, ferns, and forest debris. The hill and creek contain some large and handsome sword ferns. Cream bushes growing by the trail are pushing out leaves on the brown twigs. Soon they will be adding white flowers to the quiet beauty here.

Walking down, my lunch longing increases. I can hardly wait to sit on my favorite lake-view bench and enjoy myself, hoping the yellow sun cups will be blooming around that bench as they do every spring. They complete the ambiance of one of my favorite resting places. I see my empty bench, quicken my pace, but no. Two hikers, a man and woman, are ahead. They are there and they take my bench. These are big benches. Perhaps they will sit at one end and I can have just a tiny corner. No again! They ensconce themselves in the center, spread out for lunch and leisurely lake viewing.

A tad mollified by blooming sun cups around the path and bench, I start taking pictures of them, edging closer and closer, taking more and more pictures, until almost by the side of the interlopers. They show great concentration on lunch, ignoring me as they eat. I give up and dejectedly go along the Lake Trail. I remember a gazebo, off the trail, that I have visited without encountering others. Foiled again, it is full of picnickers with space-filling bicycles.

I continue my slow wander, longing for rest and refreshment, and soon reduced to looking for likely boulders. Near a meadow, there is a friendly rock upholstered in a covering of lichen, making it a bit warmer and softer than its bare companions. I sit, take out sandwich and water and make do while viewing a curiously crooked moss-covered oak. A passing hiker smiles and says, "Bon appetit."

My back begins to protest at this boulder perch, so I get up and walk on to see more sun cups. I go over to the now empty gazebo, but after a while, my back again insists on leaning against something solid. I hope my bench will be empty, and so it is. With a sigh, I sit, do my own lake viewing, and eat an apple.

Climbing up the trail, there are gorgeous scarlet delphiniums on the lower hill. What a sight they are, growing against dark basalt rocks and luxuriant bunch grass. Here and there, red and shining, new poison oak shoots intrude into the rocks and grass.

After my lunch adventures and flower viewing, I look

forward to the nice resting spot at the top of this hill. Only to find the bench is covered with a man and his bike. He has placed the bike so it blocks half of the bench and has over-spread the balance with his abundant self, expanding to fill space. I pass slowly, staring at him with my deadliest glance, yet he seems unaware. My sister, Edwyna, had the best ma-levolent glare ever seen. She called it "the dirty look," and it was grandly intimidating. I wish I had mastered it. He would have become thinner and neater after my glance, put his bike to the side and offered to share the bench.

I tromp on to the picnic table by the water tank, rest for a bit, then go on down through the redwoods, enjoying seeing the colors of the spent redwood needles under my feet and the fragrance of the trees and downed needles.

Reaching the entry of Two Quarry Trail, I find two cy-clists with a trail map. One is giving instructions to the other as to where to go and when to turn and how to get to his destination. The other fellow says thanks and goodbye and pedals down the trail. I ask the remaining cyclist about that trail and how many people take it, the difficulty and so on. He replies a lot more bikers than hikers use it, it's rocky to start, then widens out and is all right. I explain about the orchids and looking for flowers. He seems a bit surprised, but agrees when I say, "We are in this fine place so, whether it is looking for flowers or riding a bike, it's all good."

Farewell, Spring Creek Trail

Spring Creek Trail has some of the loveliest shaded places in Annadel Park. The lower part is heavily wooded with a few handsome redwoods along the creek. I walked there many times last year, enjoying the trees, plants and views, though the trail badly needed repairs. The first section increases in steepness gradually and, until a rocky dry creek crossing, is quite a pleasant hike. Then the steepness increases rapidly, the trail is badly eroded and rough, becoming more difficult as it climbs until its end at Lake Ilsanjo.

The difficulty and steepness of the downhill trip makes it worse than the climb up. As I completed my final round trip last year, I told myself I should not do it again. It was too steep, too hard, too many loose rocks going downhill and far too tiring for me.

In March of this year I tried walking to the creek crossing and found that extensive repairs and improvements had been made to the lower section. Feeling pleased and encouraged, I decided to go all the way to Lake Ilsanjo. Perhaps the improvements extended that far. Not so, heavy traffic and winter weather had eroded it even more and I found it to be worse and coming down, much worse.

As I started down, I met a man and woman coming up. She said to me, "Are you coming down here?" I said, "Yes, I have poles, I can do it." She said, "I hope so. Be careful. It is hard." I assured her, "I have done it before, I can do it again." Looking dubious, she added a final admonition, "Be careful."

I struggled down, wondering as I descended, am I too old to do this? My knees and hips are aching. I don't think I should be doing this as it is too difficult. And then I thought, maybe good sense will win, after all. How I hate to admit I am too old, but perhaps I am.

Determination took me down to the bottom, and I headed to the bench by Canyon Bridge. I recognized a woman there I had met the last time I walked here. I sat down and we talked of the hikes and our aches and pains. She, though much younger than I, had her share, too. After a rest, I felt well enough to go on to a short climb, to finish this hike.

I remember, while walking last year, pausing to rest at this bench and talking with a gentleman who had stopped there. We talked about how often we walked and where, agreeing we both had great enjoyment from hiking in Annadel Park. He said he was ninety-one years of age, and thought he could not continue to live if he did not have his daily walks. We started up the canyon side of the Vietnam Veteran's Trail. I told him to go ahead, as I planned to walk slowly to look at the flowers, plants and bushes growing along this trail. I noticed how fast he went up that steep, rock-filled trail.

I did not see him again until yesterday, when encountering him as he came down to the Parktrail crossing, and I was returning after the difficult ascent and descent of Spring Creek. My knees and hips were hurting, and I thought I should never, ever take that trail to Lake Ilsanjo again. Then I remembered the beautiful spring blooms of the virgin's bower clematis vines growing near the top, and began to wonder about my resolve.

While slowly going out, I looked up and there he was, starting down. He said, "Still walking?" I answered, "And you, too." We started talking, and he told me he had spent the morning in his doctor's office with x-rays and all that. The doctor told him his knees were worn out and he must stop walking. He went on to say he couldn't, as life would not be worth living if he did not have his walks. They were the best part of his days. I said I understood and felt the same way, and I did not know what I would do in a similar situation, knowing as I said it, I, like him, would continue to try to walk.

He asked me my age and where I had been. I told him and he was surprised, "All the way to the lake and back?" I replied, "Yes, and I am very tired and my joints and bones hurt, too." He went on to say he had given up that hike, but he was not yet ready to quit it all. I agreed and, wishing each other well, he went on to walk and I went home to rest.

February Hike

It is a sunny Sunday in mid-February, and there are many people out enjoying a warm, lovely time. Entering the Newanga entrance to Spring Lake, I start walking to Annadel Park. There are walkers, hikers and bikers in generous number. I cross a bridge and pass the start of Rough Go Trail. On the bank is a cluster of blue dick plants in bloom. A few feet farther there is another gathering of their small, bright blue flowers. It seems a bit early, even in this sunny location. At any time they are a delight.

Farther along, I encounter more and more white milkmaids in bloom, early beauty for flower lovers. I had seen a few two weeks ago on Richardson and North Burma Trails. A hiking group passes, going fast, engaged in loud conversation with one another. Their purpose in hiking must be to socialize and gain speed, because not a one seems aware of the fresh white blooms around them. One older man follows a few feet behind, and I say to him, "Noisy." He laughs, "Are you with the group?" "No, I am alone," I say. We both smile and go on.

After crossing the Canyon Bridge, there are more and more milkmaids, an invasion of tiny blossoms all around, white flowers sparkling against ferns on the banks and green grasses on the hills.

This is a difficult part of the trail, so rocky and steep I must look at the ground to see the best place to step, pausing occasionally to admire the surroundings and catch my breath. If I could walk faster uphill, I would not see as much. In one of my breathing breaks, I see a spot of pink to the side. I get closer and there is a sweet surprise, one small pink and perfect shooting star. I have been seeing new leaves of these plants for a while, but did not expect blossoms now.

Energized by the sight, I trudge on up. The trail is covered with numerous blobs of lava of all shapes and sizes. When I read of lava bombs thrown out by exploding volcanoes, I always think of this place. This area was bombed, bombarded, blitzed and barraged in ancient times. I have to watch my feet while going through these hills, so I see a lot of great rocks.

All-terrain search and rescue vehicles pass, going up and down this fire trail. They are complete with searchers and a search dog as they go on their missions. An Annadel Ranger drives up in his truck, waves and says, "Nice to see you." I see one rescue driver many times as he goes up and down with teams of rescuers. Each time we wave and soon are calling "hi" and "hello."

Reaching a bench, I rest for a few minutes. There is a pleasant view across a small valley and on to the distant Coast Range. It is a lovely clear blue day and, as always, turkey vultures are taking advantage of wind currents to soar and swoop above the hills. Farther and higher, a helicopter is making passes, and turns in search of a lost person. I later learn that a cyclist, off trail, had fallen and broken a leg. After a lengthy search, he was found and taken to a hospital.

I resume the climb up-hill until reaching a viewing place where there can be a fine observation of mountains marching north on the east side, the blue coast in the west and a goodly portion of the Santa Rosa plain. I see Spring Lake shining below surrounded by tree shrouded hills.

I reach the Marsh Trail, find a friendly bench, and stop for lunch. Talkative hikers pass behind me, some of them surprisingly loud. When I stand to leave, I see a fellow across the trail watching and listening to the parade of people and sound. Smilingly, he remarks, "Yackity, yackity, yackity. Sunday walkers are a noisy bunch. If I didn't need the exercise, I would never walk on Sundays." I laugh. Agreeing on the need for a bit of quiet on the trails, we proceed with our hikes.

On my way down, the friendly search driver stops, and says it is good to see me up there and doing so well. I say something about everyone can enjoy this place. He agrees and off we go, he to rescue and me to enjoy.

While going downhill, I see a bush above me and reach up to bring a branch closer. I am thrilled to see it is an oso berry bush starting to bloom. The delicate white flowers hang down in gracefully drooping clusters and, as more blooms open, the plant will be surrounded in sweet fragrance.

I am a little surprised at the number of people today who stop, say hello, nice to see you or another greeting, and ask how I am doing or if I am all right. I wonder, do these people recognize me as someone they have seen before or do I look weak, deranged, too old, what? I decide it is nice to see so many friendly faces and let it go. I think if I ever write a book about walking in these hills I will call it, "What Is She Doing Here?"

Returning to almost flat land as I near the exit from Annadel Park, I am quite dazzled by one buttercup, standing alone

in its shining yellow beauty. I stop and stand in admiration. Then, here they come again, that noisy hiking group, hurrying, talking, hurry, hurry, talk, talk. Do they ever see anything or just one another? I see the same fellow, still last in line, who asks, "Didn't I see you before?" I reply, "Yes, but I went up Canyon Trail and you must have gone up Spring Creek." He nods and hurries to catch up with the others.

I regret no one appears to have seen my glorious golden discovery and walk down the trail, remembering to pause and enjoy the pretty blue flowers I saw when coming in. I have spent four lovely hours in the park, climbing, stopping, enjoying, looking, and learning. I am a little tired, but so happy with this lovely day, I might even feel a bit younger than when I started.

Aid and Comfort

In early January, I start my walk near Spring Lake and go toward Annadel Park. There is ample evidence this is a very dry year. I see few of the tiny leaves of new plants. There are some of the tougher ones such as dock, plantain and the fillaree called stork's bill. Most of the grass is less than two inches tall, but here and there an adventurous, strong blade of four inches pushes its way through last year's crumpled, bent, dry grass.

I cross the wooden bridge that carries the trail over Spring Creek and into Annadel. On the other side a cluster of cyclists, stopped for a conference, are blocking the road. Seeing no way around, I walk forward and, as expected, they move and clear a path. As I walk on I hear someone say, "All right then, let's go uphill." Forward they go, riding on to pump and push their bikes up a hill, any hill, to have the challenge of climbing up and the joy and exhilaration of racing down.

On a hillside by the path a few blue oaks still hold some leaves. The dry remnants have changed to orange and are a colorful sight against the gray, twisted, lichen-covered trunks. The long trails of hanging fish net lichen are lifted by wind, all presented against a clear, deep-blue sky. This looks like one of October's bright blue days. All is lovely, but not correct for winter.

Stopping at the Canyon Trail bench, I sit and have a drink of water. Two women and a young girl ask about the location of trails and what to expect there. I ask where they are parked, and learn they are at the start of Richardson Trail and came down here by way of Spring Creek. I suggest they take Canyon Trail, as it will return them to their starting place. Though the trail is rocky, it has great views and fine rocks.

The girl asks about lava and, since it is all over the place, it is easy to show some to her.

I leave for Canyon, but do not go far as asthma brings on a splendid fit of coughing. A nice young girl on a bike, concerned, stops and asks if she can help, offering to assist me down the hill. Surprised, I explain between coughs, I am fine, just fine. Dubious, she offers again and I decline. Finally stifling myself, I start down and meet the three trail seekers coming up. I point out more lava and talk a bit about volcanic rocks on this trail. Enthused, the girl leads and they start hiking.

Back on flat land, I pause to admire an old oak covered with streamers of graceful lichen. I stare too long. A pleasant gentleman stops to inquire if I am all right, do I need help, offers to help me walk out, even offers his cell phone. I reiterate, I am fine, okay, have a phone, and can walk by myself. I explain I am admiring the lichen on the oaks. Doubtful, he again offers assistance and slowly leaves.

As I near the end of today's pleasant ramble, two passing horseback riders stop and a woman says, "Are you all right, would you like a ride back?" Politely declining, I say, "That is tempting. Thank you. I am fine and can finish." She cannot know I had what I consider my first and last horseback ride in 1941, and have always been content with that decision.

I must look unusually derelict today. Perhaps I should shorten my staring time. One disturbed, daft, pitiable ancient lost in the deeply forested wilds of Annadel. Alone, abandoned, at least misplaced. Oh, how sad, the poor old thing. It is pleasant to know there are those who care. I wonder if I must start to appear livelier, with purpose and be better dressed. Truly, I prefer comfort, I do not care about style, cannot be livelier, and love to gaze at trees, sky, plants, rocks, even dirt.

Yes, I am one slightly crazed old person, and I will continue to say thank you, thank you and go on with my obsessive staring. Perhaps I should always have a camera in hand, try to look purposeful, and claim to be a bird watcher.

Frogs and Flowers

I hiked North Burma Trail early last fall as far as False Lake Meadow, because I wanted to see it in autumnal mode. The dry grass had darkened to gray. Green coyote bushes gave the only color in the meadow. My ascent that day seemed to be more difficult than earlier climbs. While descending I moved slowly and carefully, testing each step going down. Arthritis is making me even slower, and I am growing stiffer, and there are days when each step becomes a test of will. During the hike I slipped twice and came close to falling.

After reaching my favorite bench, I stayed for a time, thinking about aging, thinking I should give up this trail as being too difficult for a creaky old person. Last year, I knew I could no longer walk down the upper part of Spring Creek Trail and stopped doing it. Now this trail, my favorite? One of the harder things in aging is acceptance.

I resolved to try this hike one more time in the spring, wanting to see that wonderful, flower-filled meadow again. Knowing I needed help, I asked my friend, Patrick, who runs through the hills of Annadel, to go with me.

We start up the hill on a Saturday morning in April. I think the start of the path looks even more deeply worn into the underlying sandstone than last time. We admire the creek bed with its boulders, moss, and trees. There has been so little water this past winter, few changes have been made in the size and number of limbs and logs scattered in it.

Having reached a fern bank, we stop and admire the lush ferns. The remaining water in the hill is slowly draining down and refreshing the plants. I search for white woodland stars and see a few. They are less numerous and smaller than in previous years, though equally lovely in their perfection.

There is one royal larkspur, some white foam flowers and re-markable maidenhair ferns. As we climb, we see quite a few Douglas iris in varying shades of light to dark blue, shaded to lavender and an unusual white one.

We walk into False Lake Marsh, stopping to take in the colors and abundance of what we see. The grass is green, and the colors spread in wide bands across the meadow. First, blue with orange, then a large expanse of yellow, white with pink, mixes of white, pinks, blues, then yellow butter and egg flowers, many white linanthus and others. Some of the white camas lilies remain in bloom, though most are now fading. This year I think I see more of the rare white fritillaries that make this marsh so unusual. They are small and delicate, with a light touch of blue. Each one is a visual treat. I see clumps of healthy, handsome large yellow daisies, with white fritillaries scattered among the yellows. I think these daisy-like flow-ers are helianthus. Fritillaries increase as we go into damp ground, closer to the meadow's water.

Water is running out of an underground pipe and the trail here is full of tiny frogs. Less than an inch long, they infest the grass, wriggling, leaping, and going in all directions. Patrick goes to the water where it leaves the pipe, making a shallow creek, and discovers the stream holds pollywogs and strider bugs. We are fascinated, watching and enjoying this marvel-ous place for a long time. As we go out, using care to evade the myriad frogs, we pause now and then to admire what we are seeing.

I take one long, last look, trying to absorb the beauty. Knowing I will not be here again, I want to remember all of it, to imprint myself with the wonder of this place. I need to be able to recall what I am seeing and my feelings while here. The surest thing to happen in age is the loss of your memory and thought. You may think of something or someone you love and resolve to never forget that moment, but age takes away the depth of recollection. No matter how deeply I feel this now, in time it will fade with the rest of my life.

I have been up and down this hill many times and each time saw new things. We admire the views into the canyon and see a large, rounded rock that looks as if it rolled into the embrace of the double trunks of a bay tree, or the tree grew around it, as it seems to be caught there. The rock is high enough that a little light can be seen under it. It is fascinating, but we are too far away to get a clear look. There is a recently fallen fir tree on the edge of the path with most of the needles green, and only a small portion starting to fade and dry.

My fears that my balance would not be up to this down-hill trek proved correct, and I take a soft fall after stepping on a sliding rock. I was saved from a bad tumble by Patrick catching me and pulling me upright. Each time we come to a rock-strewn, slippery section, he takes my hand and helps me down with unfailing kindness.

I am grateful to him for enabling me to have a final walk up this canyon and into False Lake Marsh during its spring bloom. I thank him and know he enjoyed seeing all those flowers, and we both were amused and fascinated by those funny little frogs.

Changes

It starts with spring, the growth of new plants, awakening of the old. Evergreen trees begin to brighten, leaves and needles seem a bit greener, twigs straighten and reach for sunlight, no longer having to lean toward the ground in winter's storms. New plants come out of the earth bending down a little, to be nearer their safe winter home. When they feel the comfort of sunlight, the caress of air, they stand straight and reach for more light and bask in sight of the warming sun.

In spring the sky has softness in its blue with occasional clouds and light showers. The new grasses hesitate as they push upward, slow to leave the safety of the dark, nurturing earth. Then, feeling the warmth, they move into it, each day a bit stronger, a little taller and greener as they rush to join the world they feel around them.

Spring is a time of color returning to paint the fields, hillsides, and forest with fresh touches, from the palest shades to the brightest. Each bloom is lovely in its own perfection. Dormant trees start opening their tightly furled leaves. Soon the leaves become larger, stronger, and their hues deepen. The nut and fruit trees push out buds, then flowers. Their perfumed blossoms will attract pollinating bees, birds and insects. Petals will soon fall and add contrasts to the grass and flowers below.

Spring plants and flowers become brighter as they begin to store seeds for next year's plants. Spring is never long enough, the time too short to luxuriate in sunlight and soft breezes. Spring is a season too brief to admire every flower, and smell the fragrances of each day and evening, before change comes to our world again.

The light rains and breezes of spring are soon gone.

As May turns to June, the days become longer and warmer. Summer's plants have more time to luxuriate in the sun as they grow. The grasses drop their seeds to dry and bleach as spring's flowers are replaced by summer changes. In spring-time everything seems green, but colorations soon show. Warm weather's blossoms can seem darker and brighter. The yellows of pears, reds of apples, and deep tints of plums are beginning. Berries are flowering as are grapes in the vine-yards, and soon their fruit will brighten and grow.

Summertime seems to become a race to the end. The crops and fruits are soon ready for harvest. Not yet prepared for autumnal changes, we cling to sunny days and long warm evenings, cherishing time spent outside with family and friends.

Then autumn comes, announcing its' arrival by shorter days, lengthening shadows, cooler evenings, and October's bright-blue sky. The bounty of summer is harvested. Fall seems to be a preparation for winter. Rush, rush, hurry, hurry, it soon will be here. Take time, pause and experience the myriad beauties of the season's changes.

Autumnal colors are spectacular, bright yellows, oranges, rusts, reds and brown and all the shades in between. As the nights grow colder, leaves slowly spin and flutter to the ground. They lie in vivid drifts and piles, blowing about a bit until a rain settles them to a layer where they darken, disintegrate and return to earth.

Darkness comes earlier at night and stays later in the morning. The wind is cooler and heavier. The rains begin again to refresh streams and rivers. Earth is ready and greets the water by eagerly taking it in. The trees, bushes and plants look better, fresher, even happier. We like the renewal, but regret saying farewell to the beauty of blue sky and fresh, white clouds.

Sometimes winter slips in unnoticed, at other times it arrives in a wet howling rush. Bare tree limbs toss and bend in the winds. Any remaining autumn flowers are downed, crushed and will soon disappear. Winter can be dark and depressing with the rain and cold. Other times it is light and lovely; the sun comes through the clouds warming the earth, and raindrops glisten on the trees and bushes. We watch the rain, thinking of lovely, soft spring and dream it back again.

Forest Fragance

On the first day of fall, I hike up North Burma Trail at Annadel Park. It rained yesterday, and I am anxious to check the moss in the canyon and on the rocks in the dry creek bed. To my delight, the moss looks fluffy and greener. I put my hand on a heavily mossed boulder and am pleased to feel how wet it is.

Looking down onto the canyon rocks, the moss appears darker and healthier. The trees by the creek carry lots of moss, and it looks good. Here is a tangle of oak trees where two oaks have partially fallen, bent almost to the ground, leaning on each other and a hapless nearby tree. A broken dead fir lies atop it all. Their moss is shaggy with moisture, and one or two tree branches are still valiantly producing leaves.

I am happy to see little gold back ferns unfurling, opening and unfolding their delicate fronds. Some remain closed, most are open, a few with slightly rolled edges. What a sight to see; these little things have such confidence that one brisk downpour will bring more rain. They may close again before fall rains return, but today they have happily revived.

There is lots of bunch grass on these hills. Though mostly dry and discolored, it always retains touches of green. Today their green blades are standing up and reaching for more damp.

Trail volunteers have been through here with shovels sometime before yesterday's downpour, cutting drainage outlets in the sides of the path. These take runoff water from the walkway to the creek below. This should prevent washouts and the deep furrows that happen every winter. The pattern of fir needles on the byway shows how much water ran down here and off to the sides. In the steeper parts the needles only

161

point one way, downhill. I am grateful to the hard workers who help preserve the trails in the park.

The fragrance of the forest has returned, and scents of wet earth, moss, bark and leaves mingle and remind me of the wonderful walks I have had in forests through many years. I pass by the mossy banks where ninebark and cream bushes grow. In springtime, this becomes a flower garden with so many kinds and colors it is a joy just to remember. I wish a bench had been placed here so I could come to sit and enjoy. Of course, it might be filled with other bewitched flower viewers.

Where Live Oak Trail begins, North Burma makes a left turn and goes up to Richardson Trail. I think of going on up Live Oak Trail, but remembering I am out of practice and will have to return to the bottom of this hill, decide to be prudent.

On a short side trip to see False Lake Marsh in summer mode, I don't go into it, just look from the edge. Now this springtime watery field is so dry it looks gray. The only colors are an occasional cluster of green coyote bushes and the deep red narrow trail that crosses the meadow. The path has cut down to the red volcanic soil and makes a bright meander through the dark grass.

Out from under the trees, I can see the sky is an autumnal blue with a few wisps of cloud overhead and small puffs of white cloud above the eastern hills. When I started this morning, the sky was not bright but had a gray look as if the weather had yet to make a decision as to what kind of day to have, clear or cloudy?

The blooms on the coyote bushes are drying and almost ready to fly. Soon there will be bits of thistledown drifting through the air in every breeze.

A small bay tree grows in full sunshine on the dry hill.

This is not a good place for these moisture loving trees. The poor thing looks unwell and the seeds are pale and withering on the tree. It looks fading and sad. Wondering if this will be its last season, I turn and am soon walking in shade with green moss and ferns nearby.

There are many black oaks here and there is one round, plump acorn fallen on the path. I pick it up and admire its size and color, brown with pale shades of purple-black, before letting it fall again.

When nearing the bottom of the hill I feel quite happy, as if I have had a fine day. Perhaps after a long, sad summer I, like the ferns, am beginning to unfold and be open to life again.